GOD'S INTENTIONAL PLANS
for Your PURPOSE

INSIGHTS FROM THE BOOK OF RUTH

GOD'S INTENTIONAL PLANS *for Your* PURPOSE

INSIGHTS FROM THE BOOK OF RUTH

by

ADRIANNE L. WATSON

Copyright © 2019 by Adrianne L. Watson
All rights reserved.

No part of this book may be reproduced in any form or by any means, electronic or mechanical, including photocopying, recording, video, or by any information or retrieval system, without prior written permission from the publisher except for the use of brief quotations in a book review.

Unless otherwise indicated, Scripture quotations are from the ESV® Bible (The Holy Bible, English Standard Version®), copyright © 2001 by Crossway, a publishing ministry of Good News Publishers. Used by permission. All rights reserved.

Some content marked MSG are taken from the Holy Bible, by Eugene H. Peterson. Copyright © 1993. Used by permission of NavPress. All rights reserved. Represented by Tyndale House Publishers, Inc.

Scriptures marked NKJV are taken from the
NEW KING JAMES VERSION (NKJV):
Scripture taken from the NEW KING JAMES VERSION®.
Copyright © 1982 by Thomas Nelson, Inc. Used by permission.
All rights reserved.

Scriptures marked NAS are taken from the
NEW AMERICAN STANDARD (NAS):
Scripture taken from the NEW AMERICAN STANDARD BIBLE®, copyright © 1960, 1962, 1963, 1968, 1971, 1972, 1973, 1975, 1977, 1995 by The Lockman Foundation. Used by permission.

Scripture quotations marked NLT are taken from the Holy Bible, New Living Translation®, second edition. Copyright © 1996, 2004 by Tyndale House Publishers, Inc., Carol Stream, Illinois 60188, used by permission of Tyndale House Publishers, Inc. All rights reserved.

Published in the United States by Uriel Press
P.O. Box 436987, Chicago, IL 60643
www.urielpress.com

ISBN 978-0-9993326-4-1 (paperback)
ISBN 978-0-9993326-5-8 (eBook)

Cover design by Laura Duffy
Book design by Astrid Lewis Reedy

Printed in the United States of America

DEDICATED TO MY DAD
WILLIE OWENS

Your life was full of purpose, and you touched and shaped the lives of many. Your influence and presence are missed.

TABLE OF CONTENTS

9   FOREWORD:
*Pastor James Womack Sr.
Destiny Church, Ft Worth, TX*

12   INTRODUCTION

22   CHAPTER 1:
Pain and Suffering

45   CHAPTER 2:
Prepare for the Journey

68   CHAPTER 3:
Purification

85   CHAPTER 4:
Restoration

95   CHAPTER 5:
Purpose

108   CONCLUSION

112   BIOGRAPHY

FOREWORD

INTENTIONAL IS A LOADED TERM. It carries with it the notion of discipline, focus, direction and sometimes intensity. Each of these words characterizes Adrianne. When my wife and I met her twenty years ago, she was and continues to be a disciplined, focused, and purposeful person. Meeting her after my matriculation at Dallas Theological Seminary, where I served as an adjunct professor, and observing her walk with God through ministry over the years has validated her Christian character and commitment to Christ. As a pastor, author, husband, and father of eight children, "God's Intentional Plans for Your Purpose" will be a unique contribution to my arsenal of books on living intentionally.

Adrianne's personal story and life experiences qualify her to share biblical insights on trusting the intentionality of Christ. When Adrianne could have thrown in the towel and given up, she persevered. She exemplifies the principles that she writes about in this book. Is life challenging for you at times? Have you encountered life delays? Are you experiencing a long-term illness or just encountered significant disappointments in life? If so, then you will benefit from this book. "God's Intentional Plans for Your Purpose" contains counsel that has been sharpened through theological training but also tempered with the pain and pressure of everyday life.

One can become hopeless after life has knocked the air out of you. "God's Intentional Plans for Your Purpose" will serve to breathe new life into you, whether you are exploring how faith fits in your life or have endured hardship. Although the biblical story of Ruth does not contain the name of God it has God's fingerprints all over it. Sound familiar? Sometimes God does not seem to be present in your life, but you can be assured He is present and able to secure, restore and direct you according to His marvelous plan for your life. Unfortunately, many have the impression that life with God should typically be comfortable and exhilarating. That's just not so. Life with God offers great promise but also contains some valleys and painful moments that may make you doubt if God has your best interest at heart. Does he really care? Is He really in control? Does serving God really matter? Adrianne answers these questions and more in this book.

This book helps you have better walk your journey. The pace of life causes one to live life at a nauseating pace at times. God speaks in a still small voice which we need to slow down to hear. Secular culture has adopted values that are empty promises, yet "God's Intentional Plans for Your Purpose" offers values that transcend time and the troubles of contemporary life. No, you won't have to travel to another land; this book clarifies your vision so you can see clearly how to navigate God's excellent plan for your life now. In

Foreword

the event you've made some bad decisions or took a wrong turn, as we all have, "God's Intentional Plans for Your Purpose" offers two chapters on God's purification and His incredible ability to restore you. In my community, organizations host Antique Car Shows in the summers. These shows encourage my heart because they remind me of God's ability to preserve and restore. In the same way, these cars have been maintained over time and restored in many instances; this book reminds us that God has a resilient purpose for our lives. Enjoy your journey through "God's Intentional Plans for Your Purpose".

PASTOR JAMES WOMACK SR.
DESTINY CHURCH
FORT WORTH, TEXAS
JUNE 2019

INTRODUCTION

FOR CHRIST FOLLOWERS—and if I may be so bold —for everyone, the road to self-discovery is really the road to discovering your unique and God-given purpose. If you don't believe in the God of the Bible or even if you are unsure of what you believe about Christianity and do not have a personal relationship with God, I challenge you to keep your mind open as you read this book. If you find yourself experiencing difficulties or your life has been filled with one discouraging disappointment after another, I want you to know that you are also reading this book at just the right time. My goals are to help you have a greater understanding of how your Creator fits into your life and prompt you to either begin or deepen your relationship with God to further discover what He has purposed just for you.

Contrary to popular belief, finding your purpose in life is not just a one-time event. What I mean is, finding your purpose evolves over time. Even if you knew as early as your childhood what you were called to do in this life, that calling will still evolve over several years so that your beginning doesn't look like the end. Your God-given purpose in life is seeded as you begin a personal relationship with the LORD Jesus Christ, accepting the fact that Jesus came to die for your sins so that you could not only be eternally free from God's wrath that comes with the penalty of being a sinner but also to live an abundant life which is a life filled with purpose. God wants to unveil Himself to you and lead you to a place of discovery. God wants you to see yourself as He sees you, understanding that when you choose to follow Him you become a member of His royal family. This book is designed to encourage you to discover and live out your royal purpose as you deepen your relationship with God in the process.

You may be doubting that you could ever really be considered royalty. For most of my life, I didn't understand the concept of seeing myself as royalty either. I didn't understand what it truly meant to be a child of God, and it has taken years for me to see myself as His daughter and princess. Oftentimes, little girls put on costumes and pretend to be little princesses. Who can blame them? The imagery of being a pink princess is pervasive in our society. We introduce the concept from infancy through the abundance of cartoons, movies, children's books, furniture, bejeweled shirts with the word "PRINCESS" on the front, princess dresses, and tiaras. Even though companies have profited greatly from the princess theme, I believe there is biblical theology hidden beneath all the greed.

In fact, royalty is in your DNA and this is your identity. I'm sure you know the Royal Family in London, England lives differently than most people. They walk in a different way, eat differently, and dress differently. Most importantly, they understand the value of their status. Well, you don't need to take a trip to England to see royalty. All you need to do is look in the mirror because you are directly related to the Creator of the universe! While nepotism is showing favoritism based on a family relationship, when it comes to you finding your purpose in life, nepotism means that you get all the perks and privileges that come with being related to the Creator! As a Christ follower, you are a child of God, a prince or princess of the King, an heir to the throne of God, a co-heir with Jesus and that in a nutshell makes you ROYALTY! When you know absolutely whose you are (Christ's), then you can begin to understand the value of who you are just as the Royal Family. That is, your identity is in the Royal Family of Christ and you belong to Him. I've also come to understand that if you belong to Christ, then you have added value to bring into this world.

I faced some negativity growing up, but I have learned that because I am a child of God, nothing anyone had to say about me even matters. My younger sister Mimi and I grew up in East Cleveland, Ohio with our loving mother and father. I must say I'm so proud of Mimi as she is an amazing woman, wife, and mother; she has always been smart. She was the Valedictorian of her high school class and is now a Senior Manager at NASA. I didn't always appreciate her intelligence though. There were times I felt inadequate and intimidated by her brilliance. Imagine the pressure growing up being compared to a "future rocket scientist." Although I never thought I was dumb, I always felt like I couldn't measure up to Mimi. Studying didn't come easy to me, and I often needed tutors while Mimi didn't struggle. She was great with math and science and is even an amazing artist. I, on the other hand, wasn't nearly as creative nor as good in school, and I had several teachers who reminded me of my lack of ability.

Introduction

As a kid, people always asked me "What do you want to be when you grow up?" I was always ready to give an answer. One particular time in elementary school I remember giving my answer like it was yesterday. Our teacher asked the entire class what we wanted to be when we grew up. With a big smile, each child began to share their dream, and I just couldn't wait for my turn. As each kid answered, she always responded with her approval. I remember squirming in my seat, so eager to share my dream. Finally, it was my turn to speak. With a big smile on my face, I stood up and belted out, "I want to be a doctor!" To my surprise, my teacher didn't share my excitement. In fact, she blurted out in front of the entire class, "Adrianne you will never be a doctor. Although you are pretty, you are not smart enough to be a doctor. Maybe you should think about becoming a teacher or just get married and be a stay-at-home mom instead." Her words completely crushed me. I sat back down in my chair as the tears streamed down my little cheeks. My teacher's disapproval was so painful. Her words, "you are not smart enough," and refrains from others saying "you are pretty, but not smart" would creep up in my mind and haunt me over and over for years to come.

I believed in those lies and that belief came with a cost. I found myself ending up in destructive and dysfunctional relationships and marriages. I accepted verbal abuse in relationships because I lacked self-worth. I didn't really understand or recognize much, if any, of my worth until I began to understand my value in the eyes of the Lord. I don't know the kind of hurt or pain you have endured or are even enduring now, but I do know your life has purpose and you are valued. I'm writing to that young child who still lives in your heart, who has been crushed by the words of your family, a teacher, a coach, a spouse or a friend. I want you to know those words were designed by the devil to destroy you and to make you think your life has no meaning. So, I will say it again—your life has a purpose, and you are valuable! God has a specific plan for your life that only you can fulfill. Therefore, one of the goals of this book is to help you erase the negative words that you've heard over the years so you can replace them with words like you are "beautiful, lovely, needed, worthy, valuable, respected, and appreciated." More importantly, I want you to replace the negative words with positive promises that come from God's vantage point as your Heavenly Father.

Your relationship with your earthly father matters. Growing up, I was often told how much I looked and acted like my dad because my father had a big heart and he "never met a stranger." I can remember riding in the car with him around the poorer areas of the city delivering food to the elderly. My dad always gave money to the homeless man on the street or to anyone who had a need. He'd even give you the coat off his back if you needed it. These images and more will stay with me for a lifetime. In fact, his acts of kindness and selflessness planted a desire in me to serve the homeless which led me to start my own homeless ministry. My father worked hard to provide for our family. There was no question that we all were the "apple of his eye." Dad liked to spoil us with lots of surprise gifts. He would often keep us guessing as to when the next gift would come and whether it would be a small, nonsense or funny item obtained at a local yard sale or dollar store or something a bit more valuable or meaningful to us individually. When we were children, Dad even gave us special nicknames. After graduating from college, I left Cleveland to move to Dallas,

Introduction

and I made sure to call home every Sunday. Dad always answered the phone calling me by his special nickname, "Hey, Little Girl!" That greeting always put a smile on my face. My dad passed away on November 14, 2016, and oh how I miss hearing him say "Hey, Little Girl!" when I call home.

I know that not everyone reading my story can say they had the same kind of relationship with their father. In fact, your father, while present and providing for your family, may have neglected you emotionally or your father may not have been present at all. Maybe it was much better when your father was not at home because he drank too much. Quite possibly your father was verbally abusive, or he was a ticking time bomb frequently exploding into an emotionally or physically abusive rage in which your mom was his punching bag, leaving you both constantly living in fear. If any of these examples describe your earthly father, then your view of fatherhood has been skewed making it difficult, or even seemingly impossible, to think of God, your Heavenly Father, as loving and intentionally good. Whether or not you experienced a loving father, an emotionally or physically abusive father, a completely absent father, or a father you couldn't wait to get away from, I want you to know that your Heavenly Father is far different from your earthly father.

Your Heavenly Father loves you, and He is here with you always. In fact, God loves you so much that He sent Jesus, His only Son to die on the cross as the perfect sacrifice to atone for your sins and my sins. Atonement was necessary because one, God is holy. Our sin separates us from God and keeps us from the life for which He created us. Two, God does not want to leave us in our sins. Through Jesus' death on the cross and resurrection to new life, we too can be resurrected from the imprisonment and condemnation of sin. We can live our lives free from the guilt and shame, as well as the natural consequences of sin here on Earth, with God's power within us; and after our bodies die, we get to live eternally with Him.

If you don't have a personal relationship with Jesus, I want you to know tomorrow is not promised for you. If you died today, do you know where you would personally spend eternity? You have the opportunity right now to receive Jesus into your life by accepting the free gift of salvation that cost Jesus his life. Will you accept God's gift of salvation today and begin a relationship with Him? If so, all you need to do is confess, in your own words, that you are a sinner and believe that Jesus died for your sins. If you do this, the Bible declares that you will be saved. God's love for you supersedes all the negative words that were ever spoken to you and all the bad experiences you may have endured with your biological father. If you want to explore your purpose, then you must process the hurt and release the pain and the baggage from your past so you can focus on discovering your God-given purpose. Remember, you belong to Christ, and you have added value to bring to this world.

God's desire for you to fulfill your purpose started centuries before you were born. God in His wonderful greatness created you as enough. You are complete and you have a purpose. Although your life may be filled with struggles, you must realize how wonderful and special you are. No matter what you've been told or what you've thought about yourself, today is the day to recognize your worth and begin living an intentional life of purpose. You may have been told you are not good enough, or you are not smart enough. You may think you are not pretty enough, or your figure is not small enough. God created you complete, unique and enough; you bring value to the world. You have something specific to contribute that only you can do.

Finding purpose must start with a greater understanding of your self-worth. Your worth is not based on your accomplishments, your bank account, the community you reside in, your ethnicity, your gender, nor your center of influence. Your value is based on your identity in Christ and what God thinks about you. Hopefully, as you read through the pages of this book, you will begin to see yourself as God sees you (regardless of what you currently see on the outside and what is going on in your life), and you will realize that you are valuable. Our society may want to tell you what to wear, where to live, what to do, how much money you should earn and what to think about yourself. You don't need to conform to what society says about you. You don't need to compromise and lower your standards for anyone and miss out on intentionally living out your purpose. You may be singled out, isolated or may even have to go it alone for a time; but if you stand firm, you can operate in the will of God and be intentional about finding your purpose.

As we look closely at the book of Ruth, we will discuss principles I believe will portray how you can find purpose even amid very difficult circumstances and life's unexpected events. Chapter one, **Pain & Suffering**, focuses on Naomi's physical struggle facing extreme circumstances that transpired within her family between the cities of Bethlehem and Moab as well as her spiritual struggle and how she viewed God as a result. Chapter two reveals Ruth's experiences as she and Naomi had to **Prepare for the Journey** to Bethlehem and endure the events that would take place after their arrival. When Naomi and Ruth returned to Bethlehem, their preparation was an important factor that would ultimately lead them both in the direction towards purpose. Chapter three is **Purification.** Purification is preparation for sanctification, which means to be set apart for God's purposes. As you embark on the journey of finding purpose, the process of purification cannot be overlooked in your life. You will also see what Ruth did to purify herself in this chapter. In chapter four, **Restoration**, you will see how Naomi's hope in God which was once lost is now restored. Chapter five is **Purpose.** This chapter will explain why understanding your purpose is important to fully utilizing your gifts when you have a relationship with God as you will see through the lives of Naomi and Ruth. The final chapter is the **Conclusion**, which ties all the chapters together to help you discover your purpose.

The book of Ruth is filled with an amazing tale of broken dreams, death, devastation, and disappointments. Although the book is named Ruth, the primary character in this story is the matriarch, Naomi. As we take a walk through the pages of Scripture, it is there we examine Naomi's journey of pain, suffering, grief, purification, and purpose. At times, it is evident that Naomi lacked faith when she displayed raw emotions of helplessness and frustration towards God. As the story develops, Naomi is also seen as a cunning mother-in-law who tries to orchestrate a plan to manipulate fate through her daughter-in-law Ruth. But by the end of the story, it becomes evident that despite Naomi's frustration and manipulation, God was working behind the scenes on her behalf to fulfill her purpose.

As you read the Bible, you find many stories of people who suffered tragedies, experienced pain, grief, and sus-

Introduction

tained loss. Many times, they trusted in God, but oftentimes they lacked faith. There are stories about people who received great blessings from their faithfulness, and there are also stories about people who were faithful yet struggled with difficult circumstances just like we do. I use examples of some of these stories to help you be able to understand and see a parallel to Naomi's story. Although Naomi faced an entirely different set of challenges than what we confront today, it doesn't mean she didn't question God. Looking at the story of the book of Ruth in more detail, you will begin to see how God was working behind the scenes by showing His love and grace for both Naomi and Ruth through a display of kindness, faithfulness, and favor amid their suffering. I want you to know that the Father is working behind the scenes in your life too. He wants to draw you to Himself, so you can intentionally live out your purpose. So, put on your seatbelt and get ready for the ride of your life to finding purpose!

Finally, a very special thanks to everyone who helped make this book a reality: my editor Anita Bapttista, Jeff Wright, Annette Leach, Pastor James Womack Sr., my Mom, my sister Mary "Mimi" Lobo, and my husband Arthur L. Watson Jr.

ADRIANNE WATSON
DALLAS, TEXAS
JUNE 2019

CHAPTER ONE
PAIN & SUFFERING

Pain – Mental or emotional suffering or torment.[1]
Suffering – To undergo or feel pain or distress.[2]

Read Ruth Chapter 1:1-22

THE BOOK OF RUTH is often described as a story that shows God's redemptive work in the lives of the main two characters in this story, Naomi and Ruth. Surprisingly, the book of Ruth never mentions the name "God," but it is clear God is working behind the scenes. The scene is set through the eyes of Naomi's life filled with loyalty, suspense, pain, suffering, romance, and purpose on the dusty roads of Bethlehem and Moab. To really understand the book of Ruth, it is important to quickly review the history between the Moabites and the Israelites. Genesis chapter 19:30-36 explains a detailed background about the conflict between the nations of Israel and Moab through the story of a man named Lot who was the nephew of the Jewish patriarch

---

[1] Pain. In dictionary.com online dictionary. Retrieved February 26, 2018, from https://www.dictionary.com/browse/pain
[2] Suffer. In dictionary.com online dictionary. Retrieved February 26, 2018, from https://www.dictionary.com/browse/suffer

Pain & Suffering

Abraham. Abraham, who is the father of the Jewish nation, was also Lot's uncle. Now I must warn you, get ready for a scandal because you may even find it hard to believe the stories that will come next in this is part of the Bible.

If Lot's name doesn't sound familiar, perhaps the cities in which he lived, Sodom and Gomorrah, may ring a bell. The cities of Sodom and Gomorrah[3] had a reputation for illicit and perverse behavior. As a result, God rained fire from heaven and burned up the cities. This forced Lot and his family to flee for their lives. They ended up in a small city in the hill country called Zoar.[4] Though they escaped, trouble would eventually follow them. Lot found himself in the midst of a scandal you wouldn't even believe was true. Lot's two daughters devised an illicit scheme to get their father drunk enough to have sex with them so they could get pregnant![5] Lot's daughters thought that if they had sex with their father, they would secure their future and continue their father's family name. Can you believe such a scandal is even recorded in the Bible? Now let's be real, Lot's daughters had to have known what they were doing was sinful. Why else would they get their father really drunk if not only to impair his judgment? Well, let me just tell you that their plan worked, and both of his daughters got pregnant. The first child born from this incestuous scandal was named Moab. Lot's son Moab became the father of the Moabites, and the Bible tells us that they were known for licentious and illicit behavior, sexual immorality and idol worship. But are you even be surprised considering that Lot's son Moab was conceived from incest and Lot's daughters grew up in the

---

3 Genesis 18:20-21, 19:24
4 Genesis 19:23
5 Genesis 19:30-38

environment of Sodom and Gomorrah?[6] For years, hostility grew between the nations of Israel and Moab. By the time the book of Ruth was written, it just so happened to be a more peaceful time between these two nations.

The events that occur in the book of Ruth are several years after the deaths of Moses and Joshua who were the leaders of the Israelites. As a result of their deaths, the twelve Israelite tribes were forced to learn how to cohabitate with each other. There were hostile nations and enemies on their borders and this was also the end of an era called the "The Judges," where the children of Israel didn't have a leader nor a king, so Judges were appointed by God to lead them.[7] Judges 2:16–21 explains the environment:

> [16] The LORD raised up judges, who saved them out of the hand of those who plundered them. [17] Yet they did not listen to their judges, for they whored after other gods and bowed down to them. They soon turned aside from the way in which their fathers had walked, who had obeyed the commandments of the LORD, and they did not do so. [18] Whenever the LORD raised up judges for them, the LORD was with the judge, and he saved them from the hand of their enemies all the days of the judge. For the LORD was moved to pity by their groaning because of those who afflicted and oppressed them. [19] But whenever the judge died, they turned back and were more corrupt than their fathers, going after other gods, serving them and bowing down to them. They did not drop any of their practices or their stubborn ways. [20] So the anger of the LORD was kindled against Israel, and he said, "Because this people have transgressed my covenant that I commanded their fathers and have not obeyed my voice, [21] I will no longer drive out before them any of the nations that Joshua left when he died.[8]

---

6 Genesis 19:1
7 Judges 2:16-21
8 Judges 2:18-22

Pain & Suffering

"In those days there was no king in Israel. Everyone did what was right in their own eyes."[9] For years the Moabites, who lived in the country of Moab, which was east of the Jordan river, influenced and coerced the Israelites with their bad behavior from despicable sexual acts to idol worship. For example, there was an incident recorded in the Bible where several Moabite women seduced the leaders of Israel, and it angered the LORD so much that God ordered Moses to hang all of those who participated.[10] Many of the Israelites turned their backs on the LORD, and they served the gods of the Moabites, the Baals, and the Asheroth.[11] Their blatant disobedience angered the LORD so much so, He stopped protecting them from their enemies. When God removed His protection, the Israelites endured national disunity, harsh economic conditions, violence, foreign oppression from neighboring countries and severe famine.

This background history is the backdrop to the first chapter in the book of Ruth. The story begins with a man named Elimelech, his wife Naomi and their two sons named Mahlon and Chilion. Naomi and Elimelech were Judahites[12] from Bethlehem. This means that Elimelech and Naomi came from the tribe of Judah which was one of the twelve tribes of Israel.[13] Bethlehem was approximately five miles south of Jerusalem. The name Bethlehem means *"a house of bread."* Ironically, there was no bread to eat in Bethlehem because the famine left the region in a tough and unbearable living condition. As a result, Elimelech packed up his family, and they relocated to the country of Moab

---
9   Judges 21:25
10 Numbers 25:1-3
11 Judges 2:13
12 Descendants of the tribe of Judah
13 Matthew 2:1

which we will find out later was probably not a wise decision. It is possible Elimelech heard there was no famine in the land of Moab. After hearing the history between the Israelites and the Moabites, you may be thinking why would Elimelech even think about moving his family to Moab? That's a good question, and frankly, we really don't know. Maybe the extreme living conditions forced Elimelech to move his family to such a despised place in spite of good judgment. The best way I can describe it would be to equate it to leaving the comforts of your home and moving your family to a place like the notorious homeless city called Skid Row located in Downtown Los Angeles, California. No one in their right mind would willfully and voluntarily move their family to such a horrible place unless certain living conditions forced their hand.

The country of Moab neighbored Bethlehem east of the Jordan river, but on foot, it was about a fifty-mile trek through very rugged roads. Elimelech and his family would eventually settle in Moab. His decision to leave Bethlehem ultimately altered the course of his entire family's life, and it also unknowingly triggered a series of unfathomable events. Soon after the family relocated to Moab, Elimelech died. Not long after Elimelech's death, his sons Mahlon and Chilion married two Moabite women named Ruth and Orpah. Within ten years of moving to Moab, both Mahlon and Chilion died leaving the women widows and in a great state of grief.[14] I'm sure this was a scary time for them. I can't even begin to imagine the grief Naomi was feeling when she lost her husband and her two sons in such a short period of time in a foreign place.

---

14 Ruth 1:1-5

When Mahlon died, Naomi was left without an heir to continue the family name because Mahlon was the rightful heir to Elimelech's property that had been left behind in Bethlehem. Since Mahlon and Ruth never had children, that would mean there was no legal heir to claim rights to the land, nor continue Mahlon's lineage.[15] Not only was this a problem, but not having children in this culture was viewed as the curse of all curses for a woman, whereas fruitfulness was considered a blessing from God. This entire scenario would have brought a sense of desperation to Naomi. To paint a picture of Naomi's desperation, let's look at the story of Sarah and Abraham.

Genesis chapter two tells us about Abraham, the father of the Jewish nation and his wife Sarah. Sarah was barren[16] and way past her childbearing years, but God had promised Abraham that a nation would come through his bloodline.[17] Sarah was so desperate to provide Abraham an heir that she asked her own husband to have sex with her personal Egyptian slave named Hagar. This way Sarah could obtain a child through her slave in an attempt to fulfill God's promise her way.[18] This feeling of desperation that drove Sarah's action might possibly be the same desperation Naomi faced as we will later see this play out in Naomi's attempt to manipulate her own circumstances through Ruth.

At this point in the story, both Elimelech and Mahlon are dead, and Ruth is childless and unable to provide Mahlon an heir to secure the land. We don't know the level of disdain Ruth was exposed to for not getting pregnant

---

15 Exodus 23:26
16 Genesis 11:30
17 Genesis 15:4-6
18 Genesis 16:3

by Mahlon, but it must have come with a heavy weight of shame, nonetheless. As a result, Naomi could not reclaim her property unless she was able to fulfill two necessary customs. First, Ruth had to marry someone who was related to Elimelech so he could purchase the land. Secondly, the relative who agreed to marry Ruth and purchase the land must also be willing to get Ruth pregnant so that she fulfilled the law to fully obtain the land. Without a husband or an heir for Mahlon through Ruth, Naomi would not be able to reclaim the land, leaving Naomi with no hope.

Naomi must have been feeling completely overwhelmed after so much loss in such a short period of time. Imagine losing your husband, both of your sons, being homeless with no financial support nor protection and being stuck in a foreign country far away from your family and friends. Naomi's emotional state was probably fragile, and her faith was challenged to the core. Naomi believed God was the reason for the death of her husband and her sons. While speaking to Orpah and Ruth, Naomi spoke these words in bitter anguish and grief, "It grieves me very much for your sakes that the hand of the LORD has gone out against me."[19] Naomi was so distraught with grief she also said, "Do not call me Naomi; call me Mara, for the Almighty has dealt very bitterly with me."[20]

Have you ever experienced an overwhelming circumstance like Naomi's where everything that could go wrong went wrong? Life is so unfair and at times, it is down-right difficult, filled with disappointments, untimely and unplanned interruptions and frustrations. Life often throws

---

19 Ruth 1:13 NKJV
20 Ruth 1:20 NKJV

Pain & Suffering

you a curve ball like a failing marriage or your spouse asking you for a divorce. The untimely death of a child or spouse, declining health, or a medical crisis are things that can completely devastate you. Life on Earth can overwhelm you with loneliness. A financial emergency or even a stressful job can make you begin spiraling downward. Circumstances can leave you wondering "Why hasn't the LORD stepped in and changed my situation?" It is important to be aware of your emotions during difficult times in life so that you do not begin to harbor anger and bitterness like Naomi. Anger causes you to become a prisoner to pain and prolonged anger eventually warps your mind such that you cannot see your life clearly. In fact, you will miss the blessings that are right in front of you. Naomi was never meant to carry the burdens of her circumstances alone because God wanted to carry those burdens for her just as the LORD wants to carry your burdens.

The Bible says, "Cast your anxieties on Him, because He cares for you."[21] God cares about your hurt, He cares about your frustration and your pain. Being angry or frustrated with Him won't change your current situation because negative emotions will eventually turn outward only hurting the people around you. So please stop being mad at God and everyone else. If you are willing, open your heart and let God know that even in your anger and frustrations you will trust Him no matter what your life looks like. If you can, try to relinquish control of your emotions and give them to God so your mind can be freed from the pain and prison you are currently in. Otherwise, if you continue to stay in this present state, you may risk losing the people

---

[21] 1 Peter 5:7

that are most important to your life, and this is exactly what could have happened to Naomi when she tried to push her daughter-in-law's away in her anguish.[22]

Even though Naomi's situation felt uncertain, that didn't mean she had to be uncertain about God. The Bible says, "Therefore do not throw away your confidence, which has a great reward. For you have need of endurance, so when you have done the will of God you may receive what is promised."[23] In other words, even in your disappointments, don't let your failures and letdowns shape your view of God because those things don't change who He is. God loves you, and He said He "will never leave you nor forsake you."[24] The Bible says, "Blessed is the man who trusts in the LORD, whose trust is the LORD."[25] This means you must dig deep and continue to trust God despite what you see in front of you because change often begins with an attitude shift, and that begins with understanding who you are. Remember, in the introduction, I told you that you are a child of God and a prince or princess of the King? Don't let your frustrations make you forget who you are!

At the height of Naomi's grief, she probably wasn't thinking everything would eventually get better. I can only imagine she also had feelings of confusion after the unexpected losses of her husband and sons. This confusion mixed with the uncertainty and likely some fear sheds light on why Naomi was upset with God and questioned why He was allowing her to endure so much heartache and pain. Naomi cried out loud saying, "I went out full, and the LORD has

---

22 Ruth 1:13
23 Hebrews 10:35
24 Hebrews 13:5
25 Jeremiah 17:7-8

brought me home again empty. Why do you call me Naomi, since the LORD has testified against me, and the Almighty has afflicted me?"[26] It was as if she was saying, "Before I left my home in Bethlehem, I had everything, but now God has taken everything away from me." Naomi was of the belief that God was the cause of both good and evil, so that meant God allowed evil upon her family. At this point, the only thing Naomi could do was focus on making a decision to secure her future. Suffering and trials are ultimately a stretch of your faith whether or not you realize it. If you dig down deep, you can find it within yourself to continue to persevere, as we will see Naomi do after acknowledging her present, uncertain understanding of God's work in her life. While you are persevering through the storms of life, there is something to be said about having an active faith. What I mean is, an active faith does not lie dormant, but intentionally seeks God when you don't understand why things are happening, and when you cannot predict what the outcome will be, and then active faith eventually transcends to trust. When you stop seeking God for direction, you begin questioning if He is causing the trials to occur in your life just like Naomi did.

As I read this part of the story, I could not make sense as to why God allowed Naomi to face the death of her family, the loss of her home and imminent starvation. It may not make sense why the Father has allowed you to suffer through your present difficulties either. Do you often wonder why we witness so many innocent people suffering? I do. In fact, it bothers me every time I see our veteran's standing on the street corners holding signs indicating they

---

26 Ruth 1:21 NKJV

need help, or when I see them sitting on the side of the road in a wheelchair under the bridge. I feel compassion towards our homeless veterans; yet at the same time, I'm angry and I want someone to answer for this atrocity. I just don't understand why our country has neglected the people who put their very lives on the line for our freedom. And why hasn't someone in our government given them the mental and financial help that is so needed? I get angry when I hear about another mass shooting like the New Zealand massacre, the Las Vegas shootings, or the senseless killings of Shady Hook Elementary school. This kind of evil will make you question why God continues to allow this to happen. In fact, it leaves you wondering why doesn't God step in and stop the evil before it happens. Unfortunately, no answer given will ever be a sufficient answer to this kind of evil. If you ever wonder if you can put your trust in a God who says He loves you[27] but is allowing tragedies, death, disease, and disappointments to occur in your life, you are probably not alone. If you are thinking, *"How can I trust God really loves me when I'm always suffering? How can I trust in a God who is silent when I need Him to give me an answer so that can I know if He is real?"* If these questions leave you in a place where you are lacking faith, are frustrated with life or have doubts, I want you to know you are in a great place.

What I mean is, if you are wondering whether you will ever be able to experience joy and happiness again, when your life has been completely turned upside down, I'm here to tell you that no matter how bad your circumstances are right now, the Father is here with you and He cares about you. God cares about your pain and your sorrow, and He

---

[27] John 3:16

is working on your behalf. Despite everything that is not going right in your life, eventually, things will work out for your good, even though right now it may not seem like it. When (not if) you are able to recognize that God is moving on your behalf, it will be an amazing testimony of His faithfulness that saw you through the very end. Your marriage may be falling apart, or you've been hopelessly single for a very long time. You may be recently divorced, or you are a grieving widow. Regardless of the state you are in, know that God is there walking beside you right in the midst of your circumstances. Whether you are in a constant struggle financially or experiencing health issues, in the middle of your trials God is there with you and walking beside you.

In this life, you will face setbacks and disappointments but there is no spiritual opposition designed to destroy you that will prevail.[28] Opposition comes in all shapes and sizes and is directed by spiritual forces of darkness to affect what you think and shape your feelings and emotions so your perspective is off and you begin to believe lies instead of truth. If you fall into the trap of believing the lies that the Enemy tells you such as "God has forgotten about you," or like Naomi, "God has brought this evil upon you," remember 2 Corinthians 10:4-5 says, "For the weapons of our warfare are not of the flesh but have divine power to destroy strongholds. We destroy arguments and every lofty opinion raised against the knowledge of God and take every thought captive to obey Christ." You must reclaim your thoughts and use the Word of God as your weapon to fight the battle in your mind to resist the lies of the devil. Stand in the mirror and remind yourself who you are—that is

---

28 Isaiah 54:17

a prince or princess of the King and a child of God.[29] Allow the peace of God "which surpasses all understanding to guard your heart and mind in Christ Jesus."[30]

Your Creator is walking with you every step of the way, and He will strengthen you during the hardest times you face. 1 Peter 5:10 says, "After you have suffered a little while, the God of all grace, who has called you to his eternal glory in Christ, will himself restore, confirm, strengthen and establish you." Although I personally know this verse to be true, I will admit there have been times I have cried out to God, questioning why He allowed the emotional pain, the disappointments and especially the physical suffering. Sometimes I've struggled with feelings of low self-esteem and low self-worth because of my health issues and I must constantly fight a battle within my mind against the lies of the devil. At times I wrestle with doubt and I second-guess myself wondering if what I'm doing in life is really having an impact on anyone, or am I just wasting my time. Other times, I get frustrated with my circumstances, when things are not going my way because I just cannot catch a break. I'll have emotional breakdowns in times when I'm frustrated with God and those closest to me. Believe me, life's circumstances get to the best of us, but that's okay. It just means that we are exactly where God wants us to be because we are processing our situation and not sitting in denial. I believe in the end, we will find purpose in all of it just like Naomi did.

Naomi's struggles are similar to another character in the Bible named Job. Job faced the deaths of his children,

---

29 Romans 8:17, Ephesians 1:3-7
30 Philippians 4:7 emphasis added

Pain & Suffering

homelessness and the loss of his wealth.[31] Yet Job was still able to find purpose and maintain his faith even in his grief. The Bible tells us Job was a good and righteous man and a man of integrity. All on one day, in just a few moments, Job lost everything—his livestock (his income), his employees, his children in simultaneous deaths, his good health, and even his wife turned on him. You might think she would have been more supportive and comforting in the middle of all that loss, but instead, she told Job, "Do you still hold fast your integrity? Curse God and die."[32] Her anger and rejection, though, did not deter Job's faith as seen in his responses, "You speak as one of the foolish women speaks. Shall we indeed accept good from God, and shall we not accept adversity?"[33]

Both Job and Naomi experienced extreme pain and grief. Yet in both the stories of Job and Naomi, God was working behind the scenes to fulfill His purpose. Job remained faithful even when things just didn't make sense. In the end, God restored the things Job lost. As you will see later in Naomi's story, despite Naomi's beliefs, God would eventually restore and rebuild Naomi's faith. So then, what should you do when a discouraging blow comes? How can you trust God is for you when your marriage or another relationship is falling apart, when you experience the devasting blow of a miscarriage, when your children get into legal trouble and are out of control, when you get laid-off unexpectedly, when you take a huge financial blow, or when you receive a discouraging health diagnosis? The only thing you can do is hold on to your faith and continue to persevere until you come out

---
31 Job 1:13-22
32 Job 2:9
33 Job 2:10 NKJV

on top. Keep fighting, keep believing, keep the faith and don't lose hope. I like the way the New Living Translation encourages Christ followers to persevere. Romans 5:3-5 says, "We can rejoice, too, when we run into problems and trials, for we know they help us develop endurance. Endurance develops strength of character, and character strengthens our confident hope of salvation and this hope will not lead to disappointment. For we know how dearly God loves us, because He has given us the Holy Spirit to fill our hearts with His love." The circumstances you are facing do not and will not change who our Creator is, nor are your trials bigger than your faith. Although your problems may seem overwhelming right now, understand this, your trials will only push you more toward your purpose.

Suffering is not just a cultural issue, but a universal issue. So, let's look at two other examples of women in the Bible who endured significant difficulties and life-altering circumstances just like Naomi and Job. These women became influential despite their hardships, and their lives have positively affected the lives of many. The first woman is Esther who was a beautiful Hebrew virgin. She was raised by her cousin Mordecai after both her parents died and was selected to be one of the virgins for King Ahasuerus's harem. The Bible states, "The king loved Esther more than all the other women, and she obtained grace and favor in his sight more than all the virgins; so, he set the royal crown upon her head and made her queen instead of Vashti."[34] Although King Ahasuerus loved Esther, it was against protocol for anyone, including the queen to approach him without first being summoned. So much so, anyone who did, even

---

34 Esther 2:17 NKJV

Queen Esther, risked being put to death.

King Ahasuerus had a ruler named Haman who put forth a decree to destroy all the Jews which meant Esther and all her people would be annihilated.[35] Esther knew approaching King Ahasuerus without being summoned could be a life-ending action, but she had no choice. She was desperate to plead for the lives of her people and was compelled to break protocol. After several days of fasting and prayer, Esther approached King Ahasuerus and found favor with him. In the end, Esther was able to help rescue the entire Hebrew community from imminent death ultimately saving their lives.[36] The second woman is a virgin teenager named Mary who became pregnant by the Holy Spirit while she was betrothed to an older man named Joseph.[37] I can imagine the people in Mary's neighborhood gossiping about her, shaming her, and perhaps assassinating her character with all kinds of salacious accusations. I can hear in my head their disdain and disbelief, "Sure Mary is pregnant by the Holy Spirit." They didn't believe Mary was carrying the Messiah in her womb. Even her own husband Joseph didn't believe her and planned to secretly divorce Mary, but God had other plans. One night the Angel of the LORD came to Joseph in a dream confirming that Mary's pregnancy actually was from the Holy Spirit.[38] The Angel of the LORD instructed Joseph to take his family and escape to Egypt for their own safety because King Herod had issued a death decree in Bethlehem ordering all boys under the age of two to be killed.[39]

---

35 Esther 3:9-15 NKJV
36 Esther 7:1-10
37 Matthew 1:18-25, Luke 1:27-38
38 Matthew 1:18-25
39 Matthew 2:16

The unkindness of others and the fact that her child was being pursued by the king, did not change Mary's path. Mary's personal reputation has ultimately been restored through Jesus' sacrifice on the cross for the sins of humanity. Both Mary and Esther lived their lives with intention and focus, resulting in their lives being influential to those around them. Esther's hardships led to saving the Jews from annihilation, and Mary's hardships led to the world accessing salvation through Jesus Christ. I say all this to say, maybe you don't realize that your hardships have a purpose that is bigger than you as they did with both Esther and Mary.

Naomi's struggle was real, her feelings of frustration were real, and your feelings and frustrations are real. Imagine you are living paycheck to paycheck and no matter what you do your life never seems to work out the way you want. Like Naomi, you may find yourself anxiously crying out to God in despair, but I want you to know you are not alone. I know this to be true because there was a period in my life when I didn't know how I would be able to put gas in my car, let alone pay my next light bill. In desperation and anguish when his life was in danger even King David cried out to God in Psalm 77 saying, "I cry aloud to God, aloud to God and He will hear me. In the day of my trouble I seek the LORD; in the night my hand is stretched out without wearying; my soul refuses to be comforted. When I remember God, I moan; when I meditate, my spirit faints. Selah You hold my eyelids open; I am so troubled that I cannot speak."[40] I've been in this same place as King David, where there was so much anguish all I could do was cry myself to sleep because the weight of my circumstances was simply

---

40 Psalm 77:1-4

Pain & Suffering

too much to bear. If you have experienced this kind of pain and grief, I want you to know the LORD doesn't allow your suffering and trials just to inflict pain. In fact, Jesus said, "In this world you will have tribulation. But take heart; I have overcome the world."[41] Yes, it is inevitable that you will face challenges, but what's important is your perspective and your response during those times of difficulty.

Enduring a lifelong illness can weigh on you heavily, all but destroying your confidence that you can make it through another day. Dealing with the constant complications of Lupus, and the side effects of prescribed medications, seven surgeries, additional hospitalizations, countless pain injections, infusions, and intermittent migraines for over the past twenty-five years with the added stress of paying for it all feels overwhelmingly difficult. There are times I have been extremely sick and ready to give up because the physical pain is intense. In addition to living with Lupus, I had one medical issue last over three years. No one could determine the cause of the excruciating pain, and nothing out of the ordinary was showing up on the MRI and CAT scan results and the medical bills were piling up. For the past twenty-five years, my health journey has been a clear test of my faith. It keeps me on my knees praying and crying out to God, often suffering in silence with my two best friends, my family and even my husband Arthur, so I wouldn't constantly be Negative Nancy or a burden. No one wants to hang around the sick person or hear you complaining about being in pain *all* the time.

While I may have been silent around the people in my life, I am not always silent with God. When I stay in prayer

---
[41] John 16:33

and in His word, I am able to grow my trust in Him despite the pain I am suffering. It really is hard to explain the effect God's living Word can have on your mindset as you face seemingly hopeless or endless circumstances. God deepens my understanding of who He is and how much He loves me while increasing my trust in His timing. The best part is God relates to me in ways that uniquely encourage and speak to me. He reminds me that He won't leave me and that He is with me even through the darkest times of my life. I'm reminded of the fourth verse of the twenty-third Psalm when David said, "Even though I walk through the shadow of death, I will fear no evil, for you are with me." God will speak uniquely to you also as you seek to know Him more and look for His encouragement in the midst of your circumstances. While God wants us to rely on Him primarily, He created us for an authentic community that loves each other well. I am so grateful for my friends, family and my husband Arthur. Their consistent prayer and continued encouragement help keep me pressing forward. God's power in me keeps me going with hope and confidence in Christ as my Healer.

My last surgery performed five months after my wedding in 2018, alleviated most of the pain. Before that surgery's success, all the surgery scars on my body were a constant reminder of each procedure, every struggle, and all the disappointing test results. But looking back, I now realize all my pain and suffering has given me the ability to persevere through the most difficult of circumstances. That is, through it all, God has remained faithful with His love for me, and those scars are constant reminders that my life is a testimony of God's intentionality because He has been with me through it all. God still has more for me to do in

Pain & Suffering

this lifetime. He wants to shine through me as I seek His purpose and share what He is teaching me in various ways. Believe me, I know it is hard to see the bright side of things when you are smack dab in the middle of a trial, but I want you to know there is a purpose in your suffering.

For example, the prophet Jeremiah was called by God to preach a message of doom, destruction, and suffering to the children of Israel because they continued to disobey God's laws against sin. Jeremiah was called the weeping prophet because he constantly cried out to God while he was suffering persecution from his own people. Imagine going to church every Sunday only to hear your pastor preach the same message of gloom and doom. This is what the children of Israel were hearing from Jeremiah day after day. They rejected Jeremiah's message because they didn't want to hear that God would not rescue them nor wipe out their oppressors as He did for their ancestors who He delivered from Pharaoh in Egypt. The children of Israel didn't want to hear that there were consequences from their years of willfully disobeying God and worshipping false gods and manmade images, so they persecuted Jeremiah and even tried to kill him. Many of the Israelites were forced into exile, placed into forced labor, and were separated from their families, yet they still rejected Jeremiah's message. They preferred to continue to believe the false prophets who told them God was going to miraculously deliver them. In fact, the Israelites thought to themselves, "God can't possibly annihilate us, we are His chosen people."[42] But Jeremiah continued to warn the Israelites that their attitudes were overly confident, and instead of being delivered, just the opposite

---
42 Jeremiah 29:1-14

was going to happen. Jeremiah prophesied that God would allow the nation to be plundered and be destroyed by Babylon. They would also suffer in exile for seventy years before God would fulfill His promise to release the Israelites from captivity and bring them to the Promised Land.[43] There was a purpose in Jeremiah's suffering in spite of the threat to his life, and even through persecution, Jeremiah saw God's faithfulness.

Naomi probably felt like she was in the middle of a "seventy-year" experience with the loss of her husband and her two sons. Do you feel like you going through your own "seventy-year" experience too? Life as you know it will never be the same when you prematurely lose your child; you experience the loss of a parent or spouse; you get laid off, or you're told you have cancer or some other life-threatening disease. When your life seems to be falling apart, it is difficult to understand why God is allowing these things to happen to you. It is so much easier to retreat and fall further away from God than to run towards Him. It is tough to try to remain hopeful that things will change in your favor especially when you have been suffering for a long time. In fact, it may look like things are only getting worse, but that's because the devil wants you to believe his lies.

You are literally at war with the devil. Therefore, the devil has plans to destroy you by destroying your peace of mind, your self-esteem, your marriage, your testimony, your reputation, your family and your relationships. But Ephesians 6:11-13 says you must, "Put on the whole armor of God, that you may be able to stand against the schemes of the devil. For we do not wrestle against flesh and blood,

---

[43] Jeremiah 29:10-14

Pain & Suffering

but against the authorities, against the cosmic powers over this present darkness, against the spiritual forces of evil in the heavenly places. Therefore, take up the whole armor of God, that you may be able to withstand in the evil day, and having done all, to stand firm." I want to make you aware that you cannot complete this journey of finding purpose without putting on your spiritual armor even during suffering. The closer you get to living out and fulfilling the purpose God has for your life, the more spiritual opposition you will continue to face.

You must continue trusting God even when you cannot see how things will get better. Your "faith is the assurance of things hoped for; the conviction of things not seen."[44] God will make a way! Hold fast to your faith and know that no matter what you see in front of you right now, you have already won the battle. Sometimes, faith requires you to "fake it till you make it" through the trial. In other words, you might have to make yourself believe things will get better until they actually do get better. You may need to pray and ask God to help your unbelief so that you can believe even though you are struggling to believe. I want you to know the trials you are facing are meant to point you to the LORD, to push you, to prune you and to prepare you for the deeper places God wants to take you on the journey of finding purpose. Regardless of the circumstances and the trials you are enduring right now, you can continue. You can persevere. You can journey well.

The Apostle James tells us to remain joyful even when you face various trials because trials not only test your faith,

---

44 Hebrews 11:1

they also cause you to grow in character.[45] I know you can make it through this difficult time. Even if you feel like God is silent, please know His silence does not mean He is absent. The Bible declares, "For those who love God all things work together for good, for those who are called according to his purpose."[46] Although Naomi may not have known it at the time, God was working all her trials for her good, just as the Lord is also working your trials for your good. You have a greater purpose to fulfill in this life regardless of the roadblocks you encounter, the disappointments you will face, the suffering you are experiencing, and the setbacks that will cause you to stumble at times because you have been destined to greatness as was Naomi.

---

45 James 1:2-3
46 Romans 8:28

CHAPTER TWO

PREPARE FOR THE JOURNEY

"Today's preparation makes tomorrow's achievement."
— Author Unknown

Read Ruth Chapter 2: 1-23

AT THE END OF CHAPTER ONE, Naomi heard there was food back in Bethlehem, and it was barley season. This news prompted Naomi to leave Moab and return to Bethlehem in search of a better life. If I were Naomi, I would have been thinking to myself, "I'm far away from all my family and friends living in this foreign country, and I don't have a husband nor any sons to take care of me. Why should I continue to live here in Moab? At least if I go back to Bethlehem, I will be amongst my own people and maybe I can find some support." Once Naomi decided to leave Moab, she insisted that Ruth and Orpah stay in Moab. Out of her grief and possibly out of desperation, Naomi's words below tell us the pain she was experiencing:

> 11-13 "Go back, my dear daughters. Why would you come with me? Do you suppose I still have sons in my womb who can become your future husbands? Go back, dear daughters - on your way,

please! I'm too old to get a husband. Why, even if I said, 'There's still hope!' and this very night got a man and had sons, can you imagine being satisfied to wait until they were grown? Would you wait that long to get married again? No, dear daughters; this is a bitter pill for me to swallow —more bitter for me than for you. God has dealt me a hard blow." ¹⁴ Again they cried openly. Orpah kissed her mother-in-law good-bye; but Ruth embraced her and held on."⁴⁷

For one last time, Orpah stopped to embrace her mother-in-law and went back to her family in Moab, but Ruth did the unexpected and refused to leave Naomi's side. Naomi urged Ruth saying,

> ¹⁵ "See your sister-in-law has gone back to her people and to her gods; return after your sister-in-law." ¹⁶ But Ruth said, "Do not urge me to leave you or to return from following you. For where you go I will go, and where you lodge I will lodge. Your people shall be my people, and your God my God. ¹⁷ Where you die I will die, and there I will be buried. May the LORD do so to me and more also if anything but death parts me from you."⁴⁸

When Naomi realized that Ruth wasn't going to leave her side, she agreed to let Ruth accompany her to Bethlehem.

Ruth didn't know her decision to stay with Naomi would seal her destiny and ultimately impact both of their futures spiritually, mentally and practically. In fact, Ruth's decision to remain gives us a preview of how God was working behind the scenes on Naomi's behalf. At the end of chapter one, the story tells us that Ruth turned from worshipping

---

47 Ruth 1:12-14 MSG
48 Ruth 1:15-18

the gods of Moab to worshipping the God of Israel. In fact, Ruth had either a spiritual conversion or a spiritual awakening when she made the decision to follow Naomi's God, the God of Israel, when she said, "Your people shall be my people, and your God my God."[49] After Ruth's husband Mahlon died, she was no longer obligated to remain with Naomi, nor was she obligated to worship Naomi's God. Yet, Ruth remained loyal to Naomi and ultimately to Naomi's God. Ruth could have been thinking to herself, "Maybe it is better to remain with Naomi than to be all alone." We could just assume Ruth realized her Moabite gods had not answered her prayers, so why not trust in Naomi's God? Or perhaps growing up in Moab, Ruth heard the stories about the children of Israel who walked on dry land through the Red Sea and perhaps this knowledge compelled her to believe in Naomi's God. Maybe all or none of these scenarios are true. Quite possibly, it was just Ruth's genuine love for her mother-in-law that was the reason why she decided to remain with Naomi. Although we do not know what made Ruth turn from her gods and stay with Naomi, we do know in that act of faith, Ruth put her trust in the God of Israel. It was Ruth's new or renewed faith that ultimately catapulted her inner strength to prepare her to tackle the journey ahead.

When you think your situation is too big for you to handle, and you are having feelings of helplessness, please know the problems you are facing as you prepare for the journey of purpose are never too big for God. Naomi was overwhelmed by grief and uncertainty, yet her situation was not too big for God. Although Moab was a constant

---

49 Ruth 1:16 NKJV

reminder to Naomi of her grief, which catapulted her decision to leave and return to Bethlehem, it was the beginning of the growth she would experience that would ultimately stretch and renew her faith. I believe, as you prepare for the journey of purpose, there is a growth process that occurs within your heart and mind, and it gets you ready for a huge blessing. Through the difficult times on the journey, God will continue to show Himself as faithful in your life as you will see through Naomi's life. Although your situation may feel unbearable, you are still unbreakable. What I mean is, God has built you for this very time, to persevere through the end of your journey. In the end, there will be a blessing waiting for you either in this lifetime or the next. Your thoughts and the words you speak while you are preparing for the journey are very important. Romans 12:2 says to "Be transformed by the renewal of your mind" because you are worth it! In other words, get rid of the junk that has been clouding your mind. Remember you are God's child. Believe it, walk in it and operate in your worth so you can find your purpose in life while you prepare for the journey. Seek God's will and watch Him elevate you to live life as a change agent for the world!

Naomi and Ruth made the arduous journey on foot from Moab to Bethlehem, and they were probably hungrier than ever, tired, dirty, sweaty and in much need of a bath from walking through the dusty roads. We don't know how many days it took for the ladies to get to Bethlehem, but we do know when they arrived, they were in need of food and shelter. It was a noble gesture for Ruth to pledge to remain by Naomi's side, but doing so meant Ruth needed to find a job and food to help provide for them both. The start of chapter two of the book of Ruth introduces a new character and shows us Ruth was not just relying on Naomi alone nor on a miracle from God. Ruth knows this journey means work, and she trusts God to provide it if she seeks it. "Naomi had a relative of her husband's, a worthy man of the clan of Elimelech, whose name was Boaz. And Ruth the Moabite said to Naomi, 'Let me go to the field and glean among the ears of grain after him in whose sight I shall find favor.' And she said to her, 'Go my daughter.'"[50] Ruth would eventually find out that the owner of the large field in whose sight she found favor was Boaz, the worthy (and handsome) man of valor who just so happened to be related to Elimelech! Coincidence? I think not! This is a reminder that even when things seem bleak, God is always working things out for your good and for His glory.

Even though Ruth was from Moab, she understood the Hebrew law made provisions for the poor and widows. Leviticus 19:9-10 commanded that the landowners not to completely harvest their fields. They were to leave some of the harvests behind so the poor and widows would be able to gather barley from it for their survival. This law was their form of social assistance. Ruth knew her position as a widow would provide work. However, sometimes we are forced to endure tough social situations as we strive to survive. It would not have been difficult to know Ruth was a foreigner when she came to Naomi's hometown. The workers would immediately notice Ruth looked and sounded different from everyone else working in the fields. Remember, the Israelites looked down on the Moabites who were known for their idol worship and sexual immorality. Ruth probably had to overcome gossiping, snickering, and finger-pointing.

---

50 Ruth 2:1-2

Ruth's foreign accent made her stand out, and her unique style of clothing possibly indicated she was a widow. Ruth's status as a foreigner would not provide many friends if any. She didn't let all these differences distract her from finding food. Ruth didn't have time for what the workers might think or say about her because she wasn't going to let them stop her from obtaining what she needed.

My sisters and brothers, there will times in life when you need to have a dose of what I like to call "spiritual amnesia." Spiritual amnesia is when you forget about your past hurts, your failures and those negative words that were spoken to you as a child and take advantage of what is right in front of you. It was as if Ruth was saying, "Too late! Don't you know I already know who I am? I know I am a Moabite. I know my heritage comes from a perverse and immoral nation. I know you probably don't care for my kind, but none of that even matters now because I am a child of God!" When your enemies want to remind you of your past, remind them who you are today! When the naysayers want to bring up your old baggage, remind them who you are! You are a child of God, a Prince or Princess of the King, and you are Royalty! So, walk in it and ignore what everyone else thinks or says and tap into your inner strength and power through the Holy Spirit. Even if your past is stained like Ruth's people from Moab, it doesn't have to keep you from living out your purpose.

Ruth knew what she needed to do, but the work of gleaning in the field would not be an easy task. The barley season was in the Spring, and the days of gleaning became warmer as the season progressed. Gleaning the field for grain meant Ruth would spend her day bending and stooping even into the late evening as she searched for leftovers, sweat dripping down her face as the day got longer and her bundles got heavier and heavier. With dry lips and a parched throat, she was forced to continue this laborious task over and over desperately searching for any grain she could find. Ruth continued to go to the field daily through the entire harvest season until it was time for the threshing of the harvest. During this time in history, harvesting was a manual process called threshing. Grain or wheat was harvested by first bundling it and then dumping it onto a hard but smooth surface called the threshing floor where the workers spread out the harvest. Then it was trampled by oxen, crushed, or beaten to separate the wheat from the chaff, the loose outer covering. Sometimes the use of a stick, hammer or winnowing fork (which was like a pitchfork), was used to toss the harvest in the air repeatedly so the breeze would blow away the chaff.

One day while Ruth was gleaning, Boaz immediately took notice of her. "And behold, Boaz came from Bethlehem. And he said to the reapers, 'The LORD be with you!' And they answered, 'The LORD bless you.' Then Boaz said to his young man who was in charge of the reapers, 'Whose young woman is this?' And the servant who was in charge of the reapers answered, 'She is the young Moabite woman, who came back with Naomi from the country of Moab.'[51] Now it is interesting to note that Ruth was referred to as the "Moabite woman." Obviously, the word of Naomi's return with the "Moabite woman" got out to the rest of the town. Boaz remembered Naomi as his distant relative Elimelech's widow, and it's conceivable that Boaz's familiarity with Naomi helped Ruth find favor, not to mention Ruth was

---

51 Ruth 2:4-6

likely a very beautiful woman because Boaz immediately noticed her.[52]

Ruth put herself in a place to receive provisions and before she knew it, she had gained favor with Boaz. After Boaz found out who she was, he directed his response directly to Ruth. "Then Boaz said to Ruth, 'Now, listen, my daughter, do not go to glean in another field or leave this one, but keep close to my young women. Let your eyes be on the field they are reaping and go after them. Have I not charged the young men not to touch you? And when you are thirsty, go to the vessels and drink what the young men have drawn.'"[53] When Ruth decided to follow Naomi's God, not only did she become a child of God, she also began to experience the favor of God! What I mean is, Boaz allowed Ruth to work in his field alongside the other young female workers instead of waiting for them to leave the leftover grain. Boaz gave Ruth a full-time job, protection from the men, and Boaz provided Ruth with water to drink.

"Now Boaz said to her at mealtime, 'Come here and eat some bread and dip your morsel in the wine.' So, she sat beside the reapers, and he passed to her roasted grain. And she ate until she was satisfied, and she had some left over."[54] Look at the favor of God! Ruth went from begging for food to being fed on the job! People often walked for miles to carry clean water, and here Boaz gave both water and food freely to Ruth right where she was. How amazing it is that God will enable other people to be a blessing to you. Even when things are difficult and when it looks like the door is being shut, God will open it for you as He did for Ruth.

---

52 Ruth 2:5
53 Ruth 2:8-9 NKJV
54 Ruth 2:14

Ruth is also an example of someone who does not make excuses for her circumstances. Instead, she takes hold of her situation. Both Ruth and Naomi went against the norm yet remained faithful to the Lord's direction. The fact Boaz noticed her, provided for her physical needs with food and water, protected her, and gave her a job with steady wages is an example of God's intentional providence and love for both Ruth and Naomi.

Most companies make you start from the bottom and work your way up as you prove your worth. In God's company, He can make you bypass the bottom and go directly to the top like Ruth. Just like gleaning the fields during the barley harvest was a daily routine, moving toward your purpose should also be part of your daily routine. You will never reach your purpose if your goals and ideas stay sitting on the shelf in your mind. Every day you've got to get up and do something about it instead of just thinking and talking about what you want to do. Even if it means you take small steps, such as writing down your goals and ideas, then do it daily. If you need to save money or get out of debt to reach your purpose, then save or pay an amount every pay period. Whatever it is you need to do, do it regularly so you can fulfill your purpose. Seek God daily through prayer and reading the Bible. Stop worrying about starting over. Stop talking about what you can't accomplish because of your age, your financial status, your debt, or your past. Stop listening to everyone who keeps telling you that you can't do this or that. Don't let your fear of failure keep you from taking the chances Ruth took. Put yourself out on a limb even if it means possible rejection. You must be willing to start the journey by stepping out in faith and walking in your purpose even when the steps don't make sense and when things don't appear to be moving in your favor. As you continue to grow in your relationship with God, your desires will begin to line up with God's purpose for your life.

Remember at the beginning of the story how distraught and frustrated Naomi was and how she cried out to God? We begin to see a shift in Naomi's attitude as things start to move in her favor:

> [19] And her mother-in-law said to her, "Where did you glean today? And where have you worked? Blessed be the man who took notice of you." So she told her mother-in-law with whom she had worked and said, "The man's name with whom I worked today is Boaz." [20] And Naomi said to her daughter-in-law, "May he be blessed by the LORD, whose kindness has not forsaken the living or the dead!" Naomi also said to her, "The man is a close relative of ours, one of our redeemers." [21] And Ruth the Moabite said, "Besides, he said to me, 'You shall keep close by my young women until they have finished all my harvest.'" [22] And Naomi said to Ruth, her daughter-in-law, "It is good, my daughter, that you go out with his young women, lest in another field you be assaulted." [23] So she kept close to the young women of Boaz, gleaning until the end of the barley and wheat harvests. And she lived with her mother-in-law."[55]

AFTER YEARS OF WORKING with constant feelings of unfulfillment and lack of appreciation, I decided I wanted to do more to live out my purpose. I had always known God had a plan for me, and I knew there was more to my life than working sixty to seventy hours a week for something that didn't motivate me. I knew I had to make drastic changes that might cost me some close relationships,

---

55 Ruth 2:19-23

friendships, my status, my job, and even my possessions. In the end, making tough choices was the best thing I've ever done toward finding and living out my purpose. In fact, in my last corporate job, I skyrocketed up to a new career ladder. Even though the position I originally took was a lower level position than my previous job, I decided to learn everything I could and quickly made a name for myself. After several months in that job, I moved up to a second position. Within five months, a position several grade levels higher than the one I was in opened up, but it required five to ten years of experience in the field. Although I only had less than one year of experience, I didn't let that stop me from applying for the position. And guess what? I got the job and outperformed everyone's expectations including my own.

I had everything I needed in that position and in fact, I was very comfortable. Within two years, I built a huge portfolio with reoccurring business; and yet even with all my success, there was always a burning desire to do more for the LORD and have more time to serve. Does that mean I wasn't serving the LORD while moving up the career ladder? No. Over the years, I have always served in ministries, and I've even worked on staff at a church. In fact, I can look back now and see how God was preparing me for what I'm doing now all along the way. For several years, I preached monthly at a women's shelter in South Dallas, never realizing that years later I would accept the call to the preaching ministry and officially become licensed to preach. Serving in that homeless ministry and working on staff at a small church helped prepare me to start my own personal ministry ministering to broken and hurting women. God didn't just prepare me through my years of service, though. During my corporate career, I learned a lot about my ability to learn quickly and gained a lot of confidence that has served me well in ministry. God uses every turn we take to prepare us for His purpose. So, when the opportunity presented itself to leave my job in Corporate America for a ministry job, I took a leap of faith and made the decision to leave my promising career. The process of leaving what was comfortable to go to the unknown was initially very scary. But when God puts a burning desire in your heart to take a big step toward fulfilling your purpose, you move past the anxiety toward faith. Fast forward to today, my relationships, my church, and my ministry are all a result of intentional choices I made which ultimately led me in the right direction toward finding my purpose.

I purposefully keep myself surrounded with people in ministry who can push me to be greater, some of which say things that are hard to hear or that I don't always agree with at first. For years I ran from even the thought of being called "minister" or "preacher" until one day my mentor Pastor E.L. Branch said to me, "Stop saying what you won't do. You are limiting the scope of what God can do in your life and in your ministry by running away from your calling." Those words were harsh, but they lit a fire under me that opened the pathway to where I am in ministry today. Now I understand the value of surrounding myself with people who will challenge me and not always agree with me so I can be stretched beyond the scope of my own mind.

God definitely used these people to challenge me, and through all my years of service, my journey of intentionally living out my true purpose compelled me to do more. God revealed a need to be "minister" to hurting women. He showed me what that could look like. I decided to step out in faith and start my own personal ministry in 2012 while pursuing a license to preach. The beginning of this next phase of my journey was not easy. Ministry is not easy; and in the beginning, I made a lot of mistakes. Many of the individuals that were with me when I started have long since left. In spite of all my mistakes and those who stopped supporting me, Royalty Ministries has grown into an international ministry that touches the hearts and lives of people all around the world. None of this would have ever happened if I had not taken the initiative to pursue my calling on the journey to find my God-given purpose in life.

You must realize Ruth didn't receive the blessings of food, water, and the job *until* she took initiative, asked about the field *and* started working it. After all the events of that day, I'm sure Ruth couldn't wait to get home to tell Naomi all that had happened. You must also realize God is more interested in your growth than He is in the blessings He will bring. Ruth needed to prepare for their survival, and that meant she had to put herself out there in spite of the unforeseen challenges to come. I want you to remember a time when you had to prepare for a situation and God's presence was so evident you knew He was at work behind the scenes. Without a spiritual conversion, the mental capacity to stay on track and the courage to take physical action to begin the journey of purpose, Ruth and Naomi possibly would have starved. Remember, they had no husbands, no protection and no consistent provisions. You too will starve from malnutrition when you don't eat from the fruits of your passions and purpose God has destined for you.

Therefore, you need to ask yourself, "What am I doing to prepare for my purpose in life?" Am I sitting around waiting for someone to recognize my abilities, or will I take a leap of faith to take chances that will alter the course of my life? Preparation is a process, or a system of steps used to lay the groundwork to achieve a specific goal while you wait. Preparation, intent, direction, and methodical planning undoubtedly helped Naomi and Ruth with the unforeseen events to come. In other words, preparation just doesn't happen accidentally but happens intentionally. The journey of purpose is life-altering when you are challenged to look past your present circumstances and you prepare to put yourself in a position to be used by God, trusting Him with every step. If you are living like the wind, blowing in different directions, and you are surrounded by unhappiness, then today is the day for you to make a decision toward intentional living.

If you have a big interview scheduled, prepare the clothes that make you feel the most confident by ironing them the night before or taking them to the cleaners a few days in advance. In simplified terms, prepare for the moment. If you desire to lose weight, then prepare by planning meals in advance and scheduling a time to exercise. You might need to hire a personal trainer or get a friend to work out with you for accountability. So, as you prepare for your day-to-day activities, I believe it is just as important for you to prepare for the day-to-day journey of your purpose and the blessings that will come along with it. Many businesses fail in the first five years in part because they fail to properly prepare for the unknown. Preparation helps you to be ready for whatever comes your way. Adaptability needed on your journey requires you to prepare for the amazing road God is going to let you experience. I dare you to get excited about the journey God will allow you to endure. In the beginning, things may seem bleak or very unclear, problems may arise, and obstacles will undoubtedly get in the way; but in the end, God will get His glory out of your situation. You will look back and see how all of it was a part of your purpose.

Ruth worked in the field with Boaz's female workers from morning till evening. At the end of the day, "she beat out what she had gleaned, and it was about an ephah of barley."[56] An ephah was "a Hebrew unit of dry measure, equal to about a bushel (35 liters)."[57] Thirty-five liters measures to about 77.16 pounds. Can you imagine that? Ruth went to the field that morning emptyhanded and came home with nearly 80 pounds of grain! I'm sure Ruth never would have imagined her day would end with not only eating until she was satisfied but also bringing home leftovers in addition to almost 80 pounds of grain.

It's absolutely amazing how Boaz was so generous to Ruth. On top of all he had done to meet her and Naomi's physical needs, he even gave her a prayer of blessings! If Ruth began to wonder why Boaz was so kind to her,[58] Boaz quickly let her know his reasoning. Boaz was completely moved by Ruth's faithfulness to Naomi. He answered Ruth saying, "All that you have done for your mother-in-law since the death of your husband has been fully told to me, and how you left your father and mother and your native land and came to a people that you did not know before. The Lord repay you for what you have done, and a full reward be given you by the Lord, the God of Israel, under whose wings you have come to take refuge!"[59] Boaz felt

---

[56] Ruth 2:17
[57] Ephah. In dictionary.com online dictionary. Retrieved March 9, 2019, from http://www.dictionary.com/browse/ephah.
[58] Ruth 2:8-13
[59] Ruth 2:11-12

compassion for Ruth and wanted to be a blessing to them both.

At the end of the day, Ruth went into the city to show her mother-in-law what she had gleaned. When Naomi saw all the grain and the leftovers, she asked Ruth, "Where did you glean today? And where have you worked? Blessed be the man who took notice of you." Boy if I was Ruth, I wouldn't be able to get home fast enough to tell Naomi what had happened in the field that day! Of course, Naomi was full of questions and excitement. How in the world did Ruth come home with almost 80 pounds of grain in one day? She had enough grain to share with Naomi plus plenty of extras to put into the pantry. That's just how God does it when He blesses you, it's always beyond what you can ask, imagine or even think! Won't He do it!!!

Before I launched my own ministry, I spent five years in seminary, countless hours of studying the Bible, serving in churches and working for different ministries. I always knew I had a calling on my life even as early as twelve years old. At that time, I wasn't clear what that calling really looked like. In my last year of college, I was compelled to enroll in seminary. Over the course of twenty-eight years, I studied and prepared for the very things I am doing today, even though in the beginning, I didn't know this would be the path I would end up on. Continuing the journey of purpose has helped me be able to touch the lives of many homeless women in Texas as well as encouraging men and women all over the world. With God, there are no limits as to what you can do and what you can accomplish through His will and the power of the Holy Spirit. Although your plight in life may not be that of a professional athlete or a motivational speaker/preacher like myself, God has destined you for greatness in some area. To reach the heights of your purpose, you must be willing to put in the time for the journey ahead.

There will be things that can push you off the journey, which can cause you to lose sight of the end goal and sidetrack you, leading you toward frustration, disillusion, or even disenchantment. Any of these things can keep you from staying on the path of your journey of purpose. I allowed my health challenges, multiple surgeries, and a lack of motivation to sidetrack me. I couldn't even see my own growth or what God was doing within the challenges because I was too focused on what was not going right at the time. The wrong focus slowed my progress significantly on the journey to my purpose. Although I got off track, I always felt the Holy Spirit pulling me, compelling me to get back on track to fulfilling my passions and being a beacon of light for God's kingdom. You may find yourself lacking direction and drive; but if you stay the course and walk in your purpose daily, you will be able to reach heights you didn't even know were available to reach, just as Naomi and Ruth did. Don't let another year pass you by where you are not living toward your purpose. As you experience difficulties, continue to seek God for understanding and strength. God will give you the ability to persevere, and He will help you endure the path you must take, and in the end, you will be victorious!

How many times have you made excuses when you did not obtain your goals? Have you ever decided to lose weight but fell off the wagon before you really got started? As I get older, I recognize it is harder to lose weight and even harder to maintain it. I always start out on fire by preparing my menu for the week and preparing my meals daily. I consistently make healthy eating choices and work out at the gym three to five times a week. I stop eating out every day, and I incorporate fruits and vegetables into my diet while cutting back on fast foods and fried foods. But somewhere in the process, I stop doing all the things I know will make me successful. Soon after, I make my first excuse not to go to the gym. I find excuses to skip workouts because I just don't want to get out of the bed or because it is cold or raining outside. I justify them with, "I'll just go tomorrow." Tomorrow turns into a week, a week turns into a month, a month turns into a year. Not only did I fail to reach my goal because I lacked consistency, but I also gained back all the weight I lost, completely falling off the weight loss wagon.

I keep trying to get back on the wagon, but I have lost motivation time and time again because, let's face it, losing weight is hard work. If I'm truthful with myself, I just don't want to give up the tasty foods I know are not the best for me. I really don't want to put in all the time and effort it takes to lose weight, and I hate being sore from working out. Not to mention, there are so many other things taking priority in my life that it's just difficult to stay on track. But aren't those just more excuses? I know I cannot continue living like this. It's not good for my health physically or mentally because my weight gain plays on my confidence and has ill effects on Lupus. So, although hitting my weight loss goal seems like it will never happen and my history of falling off the wagon is demotivating, I must get back on it and ask God to help me stay on track as many times as it takes.

If my example about weight loss doesn't speak to you, I'm sure somewhere throughout the course of your life you have gotten off the journey of your purpose and made excuses. Have you made excuses about saving money or paying off your debt, or excuses about going back to school, finishing a degree or getting a higher level of education? Perhaps you made excuses about serving in a church ministry or volunteering in your community or looking for a new job or starting a business. Does any of this sound familiar like you saying, "I'll get around to it" or "I'll start tomorrow?" If so then you will find yourself making excuses about your excuses because it is so much easier to place the blame on other people, on your circumstances, or even on lack of time and money instead of owning up to your faults. If you will be real with yourself then you will admit there is no real reason why you can't get back on track. So then, let's move past your failures and start preparing yourself for this journey, the journey of God-given purpose so that you can live life intentionally.

What excuses stop you from having a spiritual conversion, growing mentally or physically, or staying on the pathway to purpose? Is the reason behind your excuses fear of the unknown, fear of failure, fear of what others might say, fear of what others might think, guilt or even shame? To live out your journey of purpose, you must first have a spiritual conversion, or if you are already saved, a spiritual awakening like Ruth did. You must also plan and prepare mentally and physically so you can endure the trials and setbacks that will try to stop you from living out your passions on your journey to purpose. Realize that when you make excuses, you give the devil the opportunity to build up a false hope of tomorrow and empty expectations that you will reach your goals despite the excuses; when in fact, the probability is higher they will never be accomplished.

You might be wondering how you can get past making excuses and finding the motivation to stay on track for this journey. I believe God has already revealed your purpose to you, and He expects you to respond even though you don't know the full extent to what it completely looks like. So, you must start taking practical steps that can help you get back on the wagon such as stepping out in faith. Start making plans or goals that will help you move in the right direction, or even get someone to hold you accountable so you can be transparent about where you are in the process of the journey. And don't forget to keep praying, keep studying the Bible and keep asking God for help to keep you on the wagon so you can remain open to His direction. He will direct you and help you stay on track.

My high school track coach, Coach Mack, had a lot of different sayings but one of the sayings he consistently repeated continues to stick in my mind almost thirty years later, "Perfect practice makes perfect." What I interpreted this phrase to mean is to perfect something means to do something over and over, learning its various nuances and new ways of doing it well. While perfect practice makes perfect, perfect practice takes preparation. The very thing you find yourself working on daily is what you are perfecting. For example, arguably one of the best NBA basketball players of all time, Michael Jordan, was clutch at hitting free throws and final shots at the buzzer. Michael Jordan didn't have a stellar college career, and he was the third overall pick to the Bulls, with many other players picked before him. But in the offseason, Michael Jordan spent five hours a day, five days a week working solely on his free throw shot.[60] Jordan's persistence allowed him to shine brighter

---

60 Baker, Ganon. "Why was Michael Jordan so good?"
https://www.usab.com/youth/news/2010/11/why-was-michael-jordan-so-good.aspx (accessed August 3, 2017).

than any other player on the basketball court and even in the entire NBA. In fact, when Michael retired the first time, many other teams felt they had a shot to win the championship since he was no longer playing, therefore making Michael one of the biggest threats to ever step foot on the basketball court. Take a page out of Michael Jordan's book and start preparing for your journey of purpose.

The Los Angeles Times article entitled "Greatest of All Times" and published August 29, 2016 states Serena Williams "has won more singles, doubles and mixed doubles titles combined than any other pro both male or female."[61] While great genetics help, do you know the real reason this statement is true? Serena's preparation. Serena is stronger than most female tennis players. She puts herself through an intensely rigid training process with weights and cardio in addition to her normal tennis practices and matches. Serena watches hours of film to gain an advantage against her competitors that enables her to know their body language and their movements even before they react to her powerful serve. We can sum up Serena's success as genetics, skill, athleticism and ultimately her preparation for each match. But if Michael Jordan spent hours every single day on the free throw line preparing for his professional basketball career, and Serena Williams prepares by watching hours of film and physically training for her tennis matches, what are you willing to do to get ready for the things that God has destined you to do?

As you take in both Naomi and Ruth's stories through the eyes of your own life, I propose that you deliberate-

---

61 Kim, Kyle and Los Angeles Times Staff. "Greatest of All Times." https://www.latimes.com/projects/la-sp-serena-williams-greatest-all-time/ (accessed August 1, 2017).

ly think about one activity that you are passionate about that brings you the most satisfaction. It doesn't matter how old you are because if you are still breathing, then you still have purpose. Take the time to describe it while uncovering multiple ways to be deliberate about pursuing your own purpose. No, really. Now. Stop reading, get some paper or a journal and a pen or write in this section below. Write! I'll be here when you are done.

_____

_____

_____

_____

_____

_____

_____

_____

_____

_____

_____

_____

_____

_____

_____

_____

_____

Way to go! You are on your way, and every step, even the smallest, is a step forward. Now, read through each of your points and see how the activity you wrote down begins to manifest itself into your greater purpose and God's plan for your life. What other words come to mind that inspire you to live intentionally? Write them down! When something you read in this book sticks out for you, highlight it. Continue reading the stories of Naomi and Ruth with the mindset of finding God's purpose and plan for your life so you may live life intentionally. It is only fitting that, as we end this chapter, we stop to invite God to further guide your heart toward the purpose He has for you. Ask God to help you have a spiritual conversion or awakening and the mental and physical capacity you need to stay on track to finding your God-given purpose.

Pray aloud. "Heavenly Father, please help me understand this preparation process so I may live my life intentionally. Please show me the areas that are sucking up my time and robbing me from living intentionally such as social media, television, or other things that are getting in the way of me fulfilling my purpose. I don't know all the steps I need to take, but I am open and willing to Your direction and Your will. Please show me your path that will prepare me for all the wonderful things You have in store for me. Show me how to start the journey for my future and open my eyes to innovative ideas, new thought processes and new and exciting ways of looking at my life. I ask you to help me seek You as You point me down the path to intentional living. In Jesus name, Amen."

CHAPTER THREE
PURIFICATION

"As threshing purifies the wheat from the chaff, so does affection purify virtue."[62]
— Christian Nestell Bovee

Read Ruth Chapter 3:1-18

REMEMBER NAOMI'S OUTCRY at the beginning of the story in chapter one? She was filled with bitterness, grief and even told people to call her "Mara," which is translated bitter.[63] Naomi was so bitter and angry with God as she cried out to Him in anguish believing He brought calamity to her family and had turned on her. But now we are seeing a shift in Naomi's mindset. She is seeing that God did not turn on her. She says, "May he be blessed by the LORD, whose kindness has not forsaken the living or the dead!"[64] Up to this point, Naomi's life was full of challenges that could have completely taken her out, and she was at her breaking point. For the first time since the death of her husband and sons, Naomi was able to see that God was working behind the scenes on her behalf. How many times

---
62 Bovee, Christian Nestell. "Brainy Quote."
     www.brainyquote.com/quotes/christian_nestell_bovee_119248 (accessed October 3, 2018).
63 Ruth 1:20
64 Ruth 2:20

have you wanted to give up only to see a glimmer of hope and light at the end of the tunnel?

There is a phrase that the old folks at my church growing up used to say, "He may not come when you want Him, but He's always on time!" God had not forgotten about Naomi, and He certainly hasn't forgotten about you. No matter how difficult your life may be right now, if you are going to live out your purpose, then I'm here to tell you don't expect it will be easy. You will experience bumps and bruises all along the way, but those obstacles are a part of the pathway that will eventually get you to the end, which is living an intentional life filled with purpose.

Each day of the barley harvest, Ruth went to the field to work with the women while she lived with Naomi. Quite possibly Naomi began to think about what would happen to them after the barley season was over. By the end of the barley season, which lasted several months, Naomi realized that Boaz could be the avenue to ultimately provide permanent income and protection for her and Ruth. In chapter three, the scene begins with Naomi's plan to put Ruth in a position to secure a future with Boaz that would also secure her future. Oh, how I love the way the Message Bible describes this next scene:

> [1-2] "One day her mother-in-law Naomi said to Ruth, "My dear daughter, isn't it about time I arrange a good home for you, so you can have a happy life? And isn't Boaz our close relative, the one with whose young women you've been working? Maybe it's time to make our move. Tonight, is the night of Boaz's barley harvest at the threshing floor. [3-4] Take a bath. Put on some perfume. Get all dressed up and go to the threshing floor. But don't let him know you're there until the party is well under way and he's had plenty of food and drink. When you see him slipping off to sleep, watch

where he lies down and then go there. Lie at his feet to let him know you are available to him for marriage. Then wait and see what he says. He'll tell you what to do."⁶⁵

Now, wait a minute! Am I reading into this scene or could it be that Naomi was planning for Ruth to seduce Boaz into marriage? Naomi gave Ruth several commands that we will examine in more detail, and I'll let you decide. Naomi said, "My dear daughter, isn't it about time I arrange a good home for you, so you can have a happy life?"⁶⁶ Essentially Naomi was saying, "Ruth its high time I help you find you a husband." This was just the beginning of Naomi's scheme. Hebrew law, as recorded in Deuteronomy 25:5-6, extended the obligation of a brother as a legal option to the closest relative. Deuteronomy states, "If brothers dwell together, and one of them dies and has no son, the wife of the dead man shall not be married outside the family to a stranger. Her husband's brother shall go in to her and take her as his wife and perform the duty of a husband's brother to her. And the first son whom she bears shall succeed to the name of his dead brother, that his name may not be blotted out of Israel." Therefore, Naomi's closest relative had a legal option to be a "kinsman redeemer" by purchasing the family member's property to meet the "dwelling together" part of the law by marrying the widow and uphold the family name. For Naomi's scheme to work, Boaz had to agree to purchase the land that was rightfully Mahlon's, marry Ruth, and also impregnate her and raise up children to continue her husband Mahlon's name. Boaz had the wealth required

---

65 Ruth 3:1-4 MSG
66 Ruth 3:1 MSG

Purification

to purchase the land, but would he want to spend it that way? Would he want to fulfill the other duties of being a kinsman redeemer? This would be the dream of a lifetime for Ruth and Naomi. No more hard labor and scrounging around for food. Ruth was sitting on an opportunity that could end their need for stability. This could not have been a better match for Ruth because Boaz was a kind, compassionate, wealthy, and godly man. It was as if Boaz had just literally dropped down into her lap, and ladies let me tell you, it just doesn't get better than this! Ruth couldn't pass on an opportunity like this, so she agreed to follow through with Naomi's scheme.

This section of the story reminds me of the day I met my husband Arthur. After enduring a long emotionally and mentally abusive marriage that ended in divorce, I had almost given up hope of ever being in a healthy relationship, let alone being married again. I was feeling condemned and judged by my own peers in ministry about being a divorcee and somewhat felt sorry for myself. I had had a few dates after the divorce, but nothing became serious. Knowing my purpose and place in ministry, I knew I couldn't just keep dating. I just prayed and asked God to bring to me the person He wanted me to date and within a few days, God answered my prayer. One day I heard that a church in North Dallas had a full-time Christian Education position available, but you had to become a member to work for that church. Since I had decided to apply for the position, I knew that meant I should go visit the church. I decided to visit the church for their 11:00 a.m. service. I enjoyed it but wasn't sure if it was the right fit for me, so I also went to the Wednesday night service that same week. I still couldn't make up my mind, so I decided to try the 9:00 a.m.

service the following Sunday to see how the congregation's demographics were different, if at all. Now I must tell you I never even looked up the time online to verify that the service began at 9:00 a.m., I just made that assumption since the other service was at 11:00 a.m. When I arrived, it didn't dawn on me that I was late, even though the parking lot was almost completely full when I pulled up. It wasn't until I walked inside the front doors and heard the singing of praise and worship that I realized something wasn't right. That's when I stopped to ask the greeter, "What time did service begin?" and she said, "It started at 8:30."

Everyone who knows me knows that I am habitually punctual, so I immediately started to turn around to go home. But the greeter assured me that they were still in praise and worship and that I should go into the auditorium. I reluctantly agreed, and as soon as I walked through the double doors all the singing stopped and everyone sat down. I was left standing in the middle of the aisle, and I immediately went into panic mode scanning for the nearest seat. There was only one seat left in the back of the church at the end of the row. I saw that there was a handsome gentleman sitting next to it so I quietly asked him, "Can I sit here?" I was so panicked that I didn't wait for him to respond and I immediately sat down in the seat. After I calmed down, instantly a thought popped into my head, *"Hmm, that was a very handsome man I just sat down next to."* After that fleeting thought, I began paying attention to the sermon.

When it came time to open our Bibles, I noticed that the handsome man had highlighted several verses and there was his own handwriting in the margins of his Bible. I took a mental note and said to myself, *"Hmm this guy is really serious about God."* Long story short, at some point in the service, we ended up speaking to one another, and I found out that he had just gotten accepted into Dallas Theological Seminary (DTS). I knew the pastor because we both attended DTS around the same time, so I mentioned that I came to visit because I knew he had become the new pastor at that church (I didn't mention the position at that time). At the end of the service, we stayed around to chat and that's when he asked me if he could call me. Ladies, of course, I said yes!

You won't believe this, but we talked on the phone for close to three hours later that afternoon, only to find out we both lived across the street in adjacent apartment buildings! We agreed to walk to meet each other on our first unofficial date in the middle of the July heat. I decided to bring around two cold bottles of water, met him at my apartment office, and ladies the rest is history. I say all this to say, that no matter your past, no matter your history of dysfunctional relationships, divorce or singleness, God can still do the impossible. He can even drop your future husband in your lap like He did for Ruth or you may plop down next to him as I did. God was working behind the scenes for Ruth, and He was working behind the scenes for me. I found out later that my husband had been praying for God to literally bring him his wife. Arthur said to himself at the moment I sat down next to him, "Wow, the pretty girl never sits next to me!" My being late to church that Sunday was a divine appointment. God answered my husband's prayers by allowing me to literally sit next to him at church. Friends, all I can say is, "Won't God do it!" I remember having a conversation with God after Arthur and I went on a date early in our relationship in which I said, "God if Arthur is to be my husband just show me if this is Your plan for me." A year and a half later, I married a gentle, kind, godly man who is absolutely the love of my life.

There was no scheming going on between me and God on the day I met Arthur at church. But in Ruth's case, doesn't it seem like Naomi is seriously scheming a plan for Ruth to seduce Boaz into marriage to secure both of their futures? I'll let you be the judge by reminding you what Naomi said to Ruth. "Maybe it's time to make our move. Tonight, is the night of Boaz's barley harvest at the threshing floor. Take a bath. Put on some perfume. Get all dressed up and go to the threshing floor. But don't let him know you're there until the party is well under way and he's had plenty of food and drink. When you see him slipping off to sleep, watch where he lies down and then go there. Lie at his feet to let him know you are available to him for marriage."[67] Considering how the entire scene was played out in the middle of the night makes it difficult to believe that Naomi's plan was purely innocent. So, let's be real ladies, if you are planning to put on your little black dress, apply your favorite smelling perfume, wait till the man is full of food and wine and then secretly climb into his bed in the middle of the night, there is only one thing that you probably have in mind. But, let's see exactly where this story leads.

First Naomi commanded Ruth to take a bath and purify herself. Purification is a process of removing dirt, filth, and anything that contaminates. Now ladies, if you have a hot date, there is no way you would skip a shower and not get yourself cleaned up. Have you ever been on a date with someone who smelled and was dirty? I have and believe

---

[67] Ruth 3:1-4

Purification

me, that date did not last long! Despite her fatigue from the day, Ruth followed Naomi's instructions and began to purify herself. In America, we hardly ever think about the luxury of having running water to shower and bathe daily. A few years ago, I traveled to Sibasa, South Africa for my first mission trip. I was astonished to see how many of the villagers lived without running water. In fact, the women walked between 5 to 15 miles to the water well every day to retrieve and carry water back to their villages to cook and to bathe. In this time in history, regular bathing was a luxury just like it still is in many of the underdeveloped parts of the world today. No one knows how long it had been since Ruth had bathed, but it was clear that Naomi wanted Ruth to smell good.

When I think about purification in relation to reaching your purpose, I think of leaving behind any excess baggage or specific things that are holding you back. Sometimes you need to take out the trash and get rid of those things that are keeping you from reaching your purpose. If you are feeling guilt and shame from your past, you will need to purify your heart and mind so that you can fully live out your purpose. I know that this won't be an easy task, and it may take years of individual and professional counseling to undo the damage. Depending on what is holding you back from totally being set free from guilt and shame from your past, you may need more than just individual counseling, like accountability from a support group at church or even a life group.

Most importantly, you must be willing to spend time with God in prayer so that you can grow more in your knowledge and understanding of God's forgiveness of your past. Holding onto guilt and shame will only continue to damage you emotionally to the point that it paralyzes you from living out your purpose. It also makes you isolate yourself, causing you to believe the lies the devil places into your head. The Bible clearly rejects guilt and shame that the devil tries to put on you. It says, "There is no condemnation for those who belong to Christ Jesus. And because you belong to him, the power of the life-giving Spirit has freed you from the power of sin that leads to death."[68] Although the process of purification can be scary, if you want to experience the full joy of living out your purpose, you must be willing to take the steps to be made whole again.

Naomi's second command was, "Put on some perfume."[69] Good smells are always appealing, and it is interesting to note the similarities between Naomi's command to put on perfume and the story of Esther. Before Esther was prepared to meet King Ahasuerus, she endured a time of purification as described in Esther 2:12, "Now when the turn came for each young woman to go in to King Ahasuerus, after being twelve months under the regulations for the women, since this was the regular period of their beautifying, six months with oil of myrrh and six months with spices and ointments for women."[70] The word "anoint" that Naomi used is a verb that refers to applying a perfumed oil onto the body, just as it did for Esther. The need for this perfumed oil was necessary to mask body odors since there was no modern-day deodorants or perfumed body sprays and there is nothing like good smelling perfume or cologne. I remember one day years ago while wearing a new body spray, my boss stopped me as I walked past saying, "Oh my

---

68 Romans 8:1-2 NLT
69 Ruth 3:3 MSG
70 Esther 2:12

goodness, you smell so good!" He asked me what kind of perfume I was wearing so he could purchase it for his wife. The perfumed oil that Ruth applied to her skin would remove the smell of the field and make her smell pleasant to Boaz, just like the scent I was wearing was pleasant smelling to my boss.

Naomi's third command was "Get all dressed up."[71] Ladies, this would be equivalent to bringing out that perfect, little black dress. When you put it on with your perfume and makeup and you know you are looking good, it builds up your confidence. I always tell women, if you want to be married, then you cannot leave your house looking un-presentable. Don't go anywhere with your hair uncombed, your face unwashed, or wearing ragged clothes because you never know if you may run into your future husband just like I sat down next to my husband that day at church. If you've been praying for a spouse, or for God to bless you with a mate, then you should always make sure you are ready to meet him.

Jesus tells a parable in Matthew 25:1-13 about ten virgins who were waiting for the bridegroom to come. Five of the virgins put extra oil in their lamps, and the other five did not. The bridegroom took longer than was expected but when he showed up, the five who did not bring the extra oil had gone to find more oil before the flame in their lamps went out. By the time they returned, they were too late. The ceremony had begun and the door had been shut. The virgins were not prepared, and they missed their opportunity for marriage. Ladies, don't let your life resemble that of the unprepared virgins. If you know you have an opportunity

---

71 Ruth 3:3 MSG

to take a step forward to start a business, start dating, make a big decision, or find your purpose, then just do it. Take the steps necessary to be more than ready when the opportunity comes.

When Naomi commanded Ruth to dress up, she was also telling Ruth that it was time to stop mourning the death of Mahlon. It was a common practice to wear "mourning garments" for several days, months and even years after the loss of a spouse or child. After mourning the death of King David and Bathsheba's son, David changed out of his mourning clothes. "David got up from the floor, washed his face and combed his hair, put on a fresh change of clothes, then went into the sanctuary and worshiped."[72] When David changed his clothes, he signified to himself and others that he had finished his time of mourning. Dressing up as Naomi commanded, would prepare Ruth to do the same to show Boaz that she was available to remarry. Now let's think about this command in relation to your own life. Do you need to take off your mourning clothes and prepare for the blessings to be fulfilled in your purpose? No matter what you are mourning—a divorce or a breakup, the loss of a loved one, losing a job, or any other thing—it is time for you to put on fresh clothes and make yourself available for new opportunities to come.

Naomi's next command was for Ruth to "Go to the threshing floor."[73] The barley harvest season always ended with a big feast and celebration lasting several days. There was always a lot of eating and drinking at the feast.[74] Many times you would find prostitutes sitting at the threshing

---

72 2 Samuel 12:20 MSG
73 Ruth 3:3 MSG
74 Deuteronomy 16:13-15

floor entrance to entice the men,[75] and the owner of the field usually slept on the threshing floor to deter potential thieves from stealing his harvest. Naomi knew that Boaz would be there that night to protect his assets. Being at the threshing floor was Ruth's best chance to proposition Boaz, not to mention Boaz would have been in a better mood after the heavy drinking from the celebration. All of this makes you wonder what really was Naomi's motive and what would be Ruth's response? Would Ruth confirm all the accusations and gossip that was known about being a Moabite and have sex with Boaz on the threshing floor? Or would Ruth remain pure while at the threshing floor with Boaz and circumvent Naomi's plans that seem to indicate that she should seduce him?

Naomi's next command to Ruth was "Don't let him know you're there until the party is well under way and he's had plenty of food and drink."[76] This command makes Naomi's scheme look even worse than the previous commands because it could put Ruth in a very compromising position, set her up for possible rejection, or even worse, risk her and Naomi's livelihood. What if Boaz rejected Ruth's initiation and proposition then demoted her back to a widow's status in the field? What if Boaz decided to violate Ruth, thinking that she was one of the threshing floor prostitutes when he found her in his bed?

Now ladies, we all know the best time to approach a man with a request is when he is full and satisfied or in a good mood. There is no way you can send your husband on a honey-do run to the store without feeding him or taking care of his physical needs first! For example, the Bible

---

75 Hosea 9:1-2
76 Ruth 3:3 MSG

tells another story of what can happen when you wait till the man is satisfied and filled with wine. At King Herod's birthday party after much eating and drinking, he gave his wife Herodias' daughter permission to ask for anything she wanted, and he would honor it. The little girl asked her mother what she should request, and Herodias told her to ask for the head of John the Baptist. Since King Herod made a promise in front of all his guests, he had no choice but to honor it and John the Baptist was beheaded.[77] Naomi knew that Ruth's best chance was to wait until Boaz was completely satisfied and filled with wine before she approached him because he would be more willing to give her what she wanted. I know that asking a request from someone whose judgment might be impaired by being "under the influence" is definitely not the right way to go, but this was all a part of Naomi's plan.

Naomi's next command was as risky as it could get for Ruth. Naomi said, "Lie at his feet."[78] Now remember, this entire scene was playing out late into the night. So, when you hear Naomi commanding Ruth to wait until he's had a lot of food and wine to drink then slip in quietly under his covers while he is sleeping, do you not fear for the girl and the sexual overtones of what Naomi is telling her to do? I'm pretty sure that Ruth was watching Boaz the entire evening making sure she didn't go into the wrong man's bed that night! Some translations read, "Go and uncover his feet and lie down."[79] In other words, Ruth was supposed to lay there in his bed and gently awaken Boaz from his sleep by letting the breeze that reached his feet wake him up.

---

77 Matthew 14:6-12
78 Ruth 3:4 MSG
79 Ruth 3:4

Purification

Despite all of Naomi's risky demands, Ruth agreed to obey Naomi's requests and followed through with the plan. "And when Boaz had eaten and drunk, and his heart was merry, he went to lie down at the end of the heap of grain. Then she came softly and uncovered his feet and lay down. At midnight the man was startled and turned over, and behold, a woman lay at his feet!"[80] Can you even imagine what Boaz must have been thinking? I wish I could have been a fly on the wall to have seen his face when he woke up startled to see a woman lying in his bed. He was probably thinking, "Now, I know I laid down last night by myself, how in the world did this woman get into my bed and under my covers?" Have you ever fallen asleep only to wake up with your feet exposed to the cold? It quickly wakes you up, doesn't it? I'm sure Ruth had been laying there with her eyes wide open, just waiting for Boaz to wake up so she could take advantage of the moment. If she did uncover his feet, the cool air touching his skin probably startled him and woke him up.

Now put yourself in Ruth's position. Clearly, Naomi's request would not pass the moral high ground standards of Christ-likeness, and all kinds of sexual implications could be read into it. Could it be that Naomi was devising a plan for Ruth to wait till Boaz was drunk, slide into his bed to have sex and consummate their marriage so to trap him into marriage? Or was her plan truly innocent and just devised out of desperation because she believed Boaz to be an honorable man? So then, what do you do if you are in Ruth's shoes when your destiny is right in front of you? Do you honor your mother-in-law's command and take the risk of ruining your reputation and be seen as a prostitute? What

---
80 Ruth 3:7-8

would people think if they saw her leaving Boaz's bed in the middle of the night? Would Ruth risk possible rejection from Boaz when he was abruptly awakened in his sleep? What if Boaz decided that he didn't want to fulfill the law and be Ruth's kinsman-redeemer? Regardless of Naomi's motives behind her command, God's providence would supersede anything she could concoct. The Bible states, "A man's heart plans his way, but the LORD directs his steps."[81] In other words, you can plan and prepare, but ultimately God will intentionally direct your steps toward the direction of your purpose. In this instance, God was directing Ruth's steps through Naomi's misguided commands.

Naomi's last command was for Ruth to "Wait and see what he says. He'll tell you what to do."[82] When Boaz woke from his sleep, he said, "Who are you?" And she answered, "I am Ruth, your servant. Spread your wings over your servant, for you are a redeemer."[83] Remember, it is the middle of the night, and Boaz probably cannot see her face. Instead of waiting for Boaz to tell her what to do, Ruth propositioned him with some carefully chosen words. Asking Boaz to "spread his wings over her" refers to the exchanging of rings at a Jewish wedding when the man spreads a coat over the woman to symbolize he is taking her under his wing. Ruth was challenging Boaz to be an answer to her prayers by exercising his lawful duty to be her kinsman-redeemer. Ruth, risking her safety and purity, boldly told Boaz that she wanted him to marry her and fulfill his obligation. It is at this point that we no longer see Ruth as a Moabite, but as a converted and purified follower of Naomi's God.

---

81 Proverbs 16:9 NKJV
82 Ruth 3:4 MSG
83 Ruth 3:9

Purification

Ruth, who was ethnically a Moabite, exercised the rights of a Judahite because she was no longer following the god of Moab but the God of Israel.

The next part of the chapter sets us up for Ruth's blessings to come. Boaz said, "God bless you, my dear daughter! What a splendid expression of love! And when you could have had your pick of any of the young men around. And now, my dear daughter, don't you worry about a thing; I'll do all you could want or ask. Everybody in town knows what a courageous woman you are—a real prize! You're right, I am a close relative to you, but there is one even closer than I am. So, stay the rest of the night. In the morning, if he wants to exercise his customary rights and responsibilities as the closest covenant redeemer, he'll have his chance; but if he isn't interested, as God lives, I'll do it. Now go back to sleep until morning." Ruth slept at his feet until dawn, but she got up while it was still dark and wouldn't be recognized. Then Boaz said to himself, "No one must know Ruth came to the threshing floor."[84]

Ruth's proposition was risky, but it paid off. Instead of rejecting Ruth, Boaz praised her, blessed her, prayed for her, and protected her. Even when it looked like this was going to be a steamy episode, Boaz showed he was an honorable man who respected Ruth. He recognized that Ruth could have looked for a younger husband; but instead, in an act of selflessness, she chose Boaz in an effort to secure Naomi's future. As a result, Boaz declared he would do everything within his power to provide for Ruth even though there was another relative who basically had the first right to marry her. Before he could respond to her request, Boaz would

---

84 Ruth 3:10-14 MSG

need to have a conversation with the closest relative. Boaz could have taken advantage of Ruth being on the threshing floor with him alone in the dark but instead, he remained pure. He even realized no one should know Ruth slept in his bed that night which signifies he was concerned about her reputation.

Although chapter three began with a scheme filled with sexual overtones, we are relieved that it ends without the act of sexual sin. Ruth left before anyone else was awake, so she isn't seen leaving his bed, nor risking any judgment about her character or Boaz's. In this story, it isn't just Naomi's plan that pushed Ruth into purpose. It is also the fact that Boaz, under God's influence, was a man of honor and godly character that allowed Naomi's scheme to move in their favor. It is amazing how God showed up in the middle of Naomi's plan. Ruth put herself in a position to seize an opportunity to get Boaz alone by himself with a proposition for marriage.

When a once in a lifetime opportunity comes, explore all the possibilities and look at what's right in front of you. Your best years in the LORD are still ahead of you, regardless of the pain and suffering from the past. In fact, the best is yet to come! Just know that sometimes to reach your purpose, you may have to take some extreme risks. Have courage and know that godly risk will never take you down a pathway of sin. The Bible says, "Trust in the LORD with all your heart, and do not lean on your own understanding. In all your ways acknowledge him, and he will make straight your paths. Be not wise in your own eyes; fear the LORD and turn away from evil. It will be healing to your flesh and refreshment to your bones."[85]

---

85 Proverbs 3:5-8

CHAPTER FOUR
RESTORATION

Restoration — To bring back to a former, original state, or normal condition.[86]

Read Ruth 4:1-22

DO YOU REALIZE YOU ARE GOD'S CHILD, and the Bible declares you are the Father's beautiful work of art? For example, my friend Pastor Mike loves old cars. There is always at least one car sitting in his garage in the process of being restored. Some need minimal work, having dents and rust spots, while others need a complete overhaul sometimes taking him years to complete. He works on each vehicle until it looks completely new and drives better than before. After all his labor and hard work, the car is a masterpiece. As the car is to Pastor Mike, we are God's "workmanship, created in Christ Jesus for good works, which God prepared beforehand, that we should walk in them."[87] God's workmanship simply means you are "the result of labor and skill."[88] Plainly speaking, my friend, you are the result of

---

86 Restore. In dictionary.com online dictionary. Retrieved February 25, 2018, from http://www.dictionary.com/browse/restore
87 Ephesians 2:10 NKJV
88 Workmanship. In dictionary.com online dictionary. Retrieved February 26, 2018, from http://www.dictionary.com/browse/workmanship

God's purposeful and perfect labor and skill, after which when its finished product has been completely restored will resemble a beautiful work of art. We are all flawed human beings filled with shortcomings and faults, so it's a good thing God is in the business of restoration. The Father is in the process of restoring you and removing those ugly and destructive things inside you and at the same time polishing and perfecting you on the outside.

That leads me to chapter four of the Book of Ruth. You will see how God restored Naomi into a beautiful work of art although she had to endure many hardships and suffered heartache and pain. If you are facing challenges that are pushing you to your breaking point, remember life is often a series of setbacks that may cause you to question your faith and even question God like Naomi. If you are a follower of Jesus Christ, then it is inevitable that you will face opposition and spiritual attacks. Ephesians 6:12 tells us "we do not wrestle against flesh and blood, but against the rulers, against the authorities, against the cosmic powers over this present darkness, against the spiritual forces of evil in the heavenly places."[89] In other words, the devil will do everything he can to destroy you. But I want you to know your Heavenly Father knows you are hurting, and He hurts when you hurt. God knows and understands your pain, and He has not left you alone nor will He forsake you. This is not the time for you to give up and throw in the towel or lose hope.

At the beginning of the story, Naomi was in complete anguish and was very bitter. However, Naomi began showing signs of regaining her faith in the previous chapter as

---

[89] Ephesians 6:12

Restoration

she began to believe that God was working to provide for her physically and restore her faith and status. Now in chapter four, we will see Boaz eventually fulfill Ruth's request for marriage. This not only shows Naomi's hope in the middle of a hopeless situation, but it also shows that only God's plans and promises will ultimately prevail. After Ruth's proposal for marriage, Boaz could have dismissed the opportunity to do more for Ruth because he wasn't the closest relative; instead, Boaz realized he had to do whatever was necessary to seize this opportunity. Boaz needed to find Elimelech's closest relative and try to persuade him to relinquish his rights to Ruth and the property so that Boaz could marry Ruth instead.

With Naomi and Ruth's future hanging in the balance, the next morning Boaz went to the public square where he spotted Elimelech's relative in the city. Boaz pulled the relative aside and gathered ten elders as witnesses. Boaz then proceeded to have an official court case to determine if he could redeem Elimelech's land and marry Ruth. Boaz began his conversation with the relative by saying, "You know Naomi, who came back from Moab. She is selling the land that belonged to our relative Elimelech. I thought I should speak to you about it so you can redeem it if you wish. If you want the land, then buy it here in the presence of these witnesses. But if you don't want it, let me know right away, because I am next in line to redeem it after you."[90]

It's interesting to notice that Boaz didn't mention the part about marrying Ruth but started the conversation with his relative about purchasing Naomi's land. After hearing Boaz's information about the land, the relative decided

---
90 Ruth 4:3-4 NLT

that he wanted to purchase it. How would this change the course for Naomi, Ruth, and Boaz? Would this mean that Boaz would not have the opportunity to marry Ruth if the relative purchased Naomi's land and decided not to marry Ruth? Could this mean that Naomi and Ruth would spend the rest of their lives scrounging for food and provisions? I wonder how Boaz felt the moment he realized his relative wanted to purchase the land. Was he disappointed or was Boaz determined to get his woman?

This was a critical roadblock that Boaz was facing. When I read this story for the first time, I began to wonder was Boaz freaking out or was he stressed out when the relative said he wanted to purchase the land? And that reminded me if you are in a stressful situation, you cannot let fear and adversity keep you from responding to the Holy Spirit's prodding. Fear restrains you from fulfilling your purpose, and fear will make you doubt the goodness and faithfulness of God. You must keep trusting God despite what you see in front of you because He will provide the words and direction just as He did for Boaz.

Whether or not Boaz predicted the relative's response as he planned, God provided the words to turn this cut and dry proceeding on its end. After the relative agreed to purchase the land, Boaz revealed the rest of the requirements. Boaz said, "You do realize, don't you that when you buy the field from Naomi, you also get Ruth the Moabite, the widow of our dead relative, along with the redeemer responsibility to have children with her to carry on the family inheritance."[91] I'm sure the relative didn't realize that by purchasing the land he would gain a wife and an obligation

---

91 Ruth 4:5 MSG

to father a child. It is possible, after hearing this news, he didn't want to go back home and explain to his people why he was marrying a Moabite. It is also possible the relative just didn't want all that responsibility. Interestingly, the relative's response was quick, "I can't redeem it," the family redeemer replied, 'because this might endanger my own estate. You redeem the land; I cannot do it.' Now in those days it was the custom in Israel for anyone transferring a right of purchase to remove his sandal and hand it to the other party. This publicly validated the transaction. So, the other family redeemer drew off his sandal as he said to Boaz, 'You buy the land.'"[92]

After the legal transaction was complete, Boaz declared his marriage to Ruth in the presence of the relative and the elders by saying, "You are witnesses this day that I have bought from the hand of Naomi all that belonged to Elimelech and all that belonged to Chilion and Mahlon. Also Ruth the Moabite, the widow of Mahlon, I have bought to be my wife to perpetuate the name of the dead in his inheritance."[93] Boaz was intentional in revealing his plan to redeem Ruth, and his actions remind me of the promise God made to the children of Israel in Jeremiah 29:11. It states, "I know what I am doing. I have it all planned out—plans to take care of you, not to abandon you, plans to give you the future you hope for."[94] Boaz, by God's plan, promised to take care of Ruth, not to abandon her, and to provide a future for her and Naomi. God also has specific plans for your life. He will take care of you and provide a future for you. The Bible tells us to, "Rejoice in hope, be

---
92 Ruth 4:6 NLT
93 Ruth 4:9-10
94 Jeremiah 29:11 MSG

patient in tribulation, be constant in prayer."[95] So then, ask yourself this question, "Am I praying in the midst of my trials, and am I being patient enough to see my purpose in life through the midst of it all?"

If you continue to endure, eventually you will see the disappointments and failures were all a part of the process of you being restored into that beautiful work of art. Disappointments, failure, and even set-backs will ultimately point you in the direction that leads to your God-given purpose. Even while you are in search of answers, you must continue to persevere patiently. In time, you will be restored. Don't discount this part of your journey no matter how difficult it is right now. While God is restoring you, He is positioning you for the better things to come and in the end, you will look more like God as He pushes you toward your purpose.

The dictionary's definition of restore is to "bring back to a former original or normal condition."[96] When God is restoring you, He is removing old rusted out parts like guilt, shame, low self-esteem or unresolved anger and replacing them with new parts like joy, peace, hope, and strength. These qualities are evidence that you are on track toward finding your purpose. I'm not going to pretend that the process of being restored feels good. In fact, when you are experiencing restoration, it may be one of the most difficult and painful times you may face. Some people refer to the restoration process as being gracefully broken. In other words, God is breaking away those things that are not a part of His plan for you. He is shaping you and molding you so you become that beautiful work of art. The pain

---

[95] Romans 12:12
[96] Restore. In dictionary.com online dictionary. Retrieved February 25, 2018, from http://www.dictionary.com/browse/restore

you experience at times may make you unsure if you even believe in this whole "God thing." If you are searching for answers, even if you are just unsure about what you believe right now, my friend I want you to know you are in the right place. You have not been reading this book by chance.

In fact, you have a divine appointment with God on this journey of finding your purpose and that will be a result of your restoration process. What I mean is, you have an opportunity to believe God is exactly who He says He is. God absolutely loves you. Can you imagine loving someone who lies, cheats, steals, murders, sins against you, ignores you, hates you and turns his/her back on you? Neither can I. But this is the kind of love that God has for you and therefore He sacrificed His Son Jesus for you. John 3:16 says, "For God so loved the world, that He gave His only Son, that whoever believes in Him should not perish but have eternal life." Isaiah 53:5 says, Jesus "was pierced for our transgressions; he was crushed for our iniquities; upon him was the chastisement that brought us peace, and with his wounds we are healed." Romans 5:8 says, "God shows His love for us in that while we were still sinners, Christ died for us." Ephesians 1:5 says, "In love He predestined us for adoption to Himself as sons through Jesus Christ, according to the purpose of His will." And Romans 8:29 says, "For those whom He foreknew He also predestined to be conformed to the image of His Son."

God put His Son Jesus' life on the line for you; and if you choose to believe that He died for your sins, you will be saved from your sins. You are invited to be in a relationship with Him because He has a plan and a purpose for your life. God predestined you to have a purpose and to fulfill it in your life so the world would be able to benefit from it. God designed you to connect with other Christians who are also on their own journey of finding purpose so you can encourage them while you walk through this journey. You are here to remind them that although God is restoring you, He is also working behind the scenes to point you towards your purpose. God wants you to know Him intimately, even if it means enduring suffering and challenges. He wants you to grow in your relationship with Him so ultimately you may look more like Him.

Remember, "We are God's masterpiece. He has created us anew in Christ Jesus, so we can do the good things He planned for us long ago."[97] God was intentional when He designed you. The specific plan He has destined for you to fulfill was decided even before you were born. No matter what, don't let the circumstances of your life make you lose heart and turn away from fulfilling your purpose. If your goals seem to be filled with insurmountable obstacles, then dream bigger! If you aim for the stars and you hit the moon, you are still winning! Now I will admit, I don't like it when God is allowing disappointments and setbacks to restore me either. What would my life be like if I didn't realize I was destined to do remarkable things? For one thing, I wouldn't have written this book to share how God is intentionally pushing you toward your purpose through restoration. No matter what mistakes you have made, no matter how many stumbling blocks you have encountered, you will miss out on what God has for you if you give up now. So, don't give up! Continue to seek God for guidance so you can find your true purpose and live an intentional life.

---

[97] Ephesians 2:10 NLT

Restoration

As we saw through the lives of Queen Esther, the Virgin Mary, Job, Jeremiah, Naomi, Ruth, and Boaz, that purpose is never absent of adversity and adversity is never absent of purpose. Seeking God through adversity helps you be able to see what God wants you to learn and how you can grow, which will lead to a better understanding of the purposes He has for you. A life absent of roadblocks, U-turns, bumps in the road and disappointments is a life we will never know until we spend eternity with God in heaven. So then, instead of being anxious or frustrated as you seek answers, remember that God has a purpose built within the adversity. When life takes a turn you don't expect, no matter how difficult, don't let your thoughts go into dark places and cause you to get stuck in the rut of negative or destructive beliefs and behaviors. Unplanned interruptions, no matter how difficult, can be woven into God's plan and most importantly can remind you God is ultimately in control.

Hold on to hope even if your life is filled with questions. It may feel as if God will never give the answers you seek. Have you considered that maybe the things you have been praying about are not the blessings the Father has planned for you? Could it possibly be that your prayers haven't been answered because they won't point you toward your purpose? The things you have been praying for may not even be big enough for what God has in store for you! Naomi had no clue her suffering would ultimately lead toward her purpose that we later see was much bigger than she could have imagined. I believe part of Naomi's purpose was to see and understand God in a different light. That is, God wasn't causing evil upon Naomi as she said in chapter one. In fact, although God allowed Naomi to face adversity, He was working things out behind the scenes to provide for her future in spite of her manipulation, anger, and doubt. Naomi's purpose was ultimately fulfilled through the birth of Ruth and Boaz's child, which became her grandchild.

Quite possibly, the life events you perceive negatively are there to shield you from going down the wrong path, or as in Naomi's case, to move her back to Bethlehem. Remember, your Heavenly Father knows exactly what is best for you. My suggestion is to keep seeking your purpose despite your questions and frustrations. Even if what you are going through right now seems hopeless, like Naomi's situation, hope IS on the horizon. Keep seeking the Father, keep worshipping Him, and keep trusting He will guide you even during chaotic and heartbreaking times. Instead of focusing on your pain and your disappointments, focus on the fact you have made it this far. You are still here, and you haven't thrown in the towel. Naomi's story was not over, and your story is not over. God was not finished with her, and He is not finished with you either!

The Bible says, "this light momentary affliction is preparing for us an eternal weight of glory beyond all comparison."[98] Remember, the beautiful masterpiece that you are is rooted in your restoration. Whatever pain, loss, or distress is manifesting itself right now, God is faithfully and skillfully transforming you because "no eye has seen, nor ear heard, nor the heart of man imagined, what God has prepared for those who love Him."[99] The Bible declares "For we know for those who love God all things work together for good, for those who are called according to His purpose."[100] In other words, eventually, everything will work itself out.

---

98 2 Corinthians 4:17
99 1 Corinthians 2:9
100 Romans 8:28

CHAPTER FIVE
PURPOSE

---

*"The meaning of life is to find your gift.
The purpose in life is to give it away."*
— Anonymous

CHAPTER FOUR ENDS with the excitement of hopes becoming reality. "Boaz married Ruth. She became his wife. Boaz slept with her. By GOD's gracious gift she conceived and had a son. The town women said to Naomi, 'Blessed be to GOD! He didn't leave you without a family to carry on your life. May this baby grow up to be famous in Israel! He'll make you young again!'"[101] Ruth and Boaz had a son named Obed. Obed is the grandfather of King David, and King David is in the lineage of our Savior Jesus, the Christ! Although Naomi's future looked bleak when her husband Elimelech died, God's intentional providence superseded her circumstances. Through the kindness and honor of Boaz, Ruth and Naomi found stability. Trials should ultimately point you to God, and to truly find purpose in the middle of your trials, you must have a connection with Him. The Father designed humankind to be in relationship with Him. So, if you feel a void in your heart, it is there

---
101 Ruth 4:13-15 MSG

because God desires to have a connection with you. The dictionary defines purpose as a "reason in which something exists or is made."[102] With that understanding, God created you to fulfill a specific relationship with Him that propels His ultimate purpose forward in a specific way—giving your life purpose within His eternal plans.

Although Naomi didn't realize it, God used her to ultimately fulfill His purpose and promise of a Savior. The book of Ruth started out with Naomi crying out in bitter anguish only to end with Naomi glowing and basking in awe of her grandchild. The women said to Naomi, "Blessed be to God! He didn't leave you without family to carry on your life. May this baby grow up to be famous in Israel! He'll make you young again! He'll take care of you in old age. And this daughter-in-law who has brought him into the world and loves you so much, why, she's worth more to you than seven sons! Naomi took the baby and held him in her arms, cuddling him, cooing over him, waiting on him hand and foot."[103] What a turnaround for Naomi; this was like a rags-to-riches story!

Do you know God has a plan and purpose that is bigger than you and me? God's ultimate plan is to reconcile and redeem humanity through Jesus' sacrifice and death on the cross for the sins of all humanity. In spite of all that pain and suffering, God used Naomi as a conduit for His purpose. Second Corinthians 5:17 states, "If anyone is in Christ, he is a new creation. The old has passed away; behold, the new has come." In other words, as a Christ follower, God's plan of redemption and reconciliation is working through

---

[102] Purpose. In dictionary.com online dictionary. Retrieved January 17, 2019, from http://www.dictionary.com/browse/purpose
[103] Ruth 4:14-16 MSG

your life, daily pushing you to maximize your potential. Everything in your life has a purpose because the LORD has destined something greater for you. What I mean is, God created you and Naomi for purpose, that is to change lives and alter the course of humanity.

Nelson Mandela fought for justice and freedom for South Africans and opposed apartheid. Florence Nightingale revolutionized the medical industry because of her experience treating wounded soldiers. Martin Luther King, Jr. invigorated change in the lives of African Americans and minorities by paving the way to racial freedom and equality ultimately costing him his life. Malala Yousafzai defied threats from the Taliban to campaign for women and girls to have equal rights to education. The list of people who maximized their lives and lived out their purpose is very long, but it's missing your name! *"Yeah, right,"* you may be thinking, *"I'll never be the next Nelson Mandela or Malala Yousafzai."* Regardless of what you think, God specifically has a purpose and a plan for your life, no matter how big or how small it may seem. We each need to realize the interruptions and setbacks of life will push us to a greater appreciation of our purpose. For example, on September 5, 1980, Candice Lightner founded the organization Mothers Against Drunk Driving after her thirteen-year-old daughter was killed by a drunk driver. Now her organization aids thousands of families victimized by the crimes of individuals driving under the influence. Yes, Candice went through a horrifying experience, and I would never minimize her pain, but despite her grief, she birthed an organization that has serviced thousands of victims. The Bible says, "The purpose in a man's heart is like deep water, but a man of understanding will draw it out."[104] If you want to find your purpose in life, you must be intentional about seeking God for guidance and direction. It doesn't matter how young you are or how old you are; your life can always impact and greatly influence the world.

If you are thinking, *"Adrianne, that's easy for you to say, but you don't understand what I am going through."* You are right. I don't know what you are experiencing. I don't know your individual story, but I do know my own story. A few years ago, I lost just about everything that was important to me within five months. My dad passed away, I experienced a divorce, and I was forced to find another job across town which meant leaving my church. My home went into foreclosure, I had no place to live, a very close friend died from cancer, and a twenty-one-year friendship became strained to the point of non-existence. After all of that, I received another bad health diagnosis. I'll admit those five months were the hardest and darkest months of my adult life. At times, it was very hard to keep going, yet I continued to persevere and walk in my purpose despite my losses, my hurt, my brokenness, my confusion, and my pain. I refused to let the devil destroy me nor allow my circumstances to paralyze me and keep me from maximizing my potential. I continued through it all to serve God with the gifts He has given me. I stayed on my face crying out to God, praying fervently and seeking the Holy Spirit's power in my life to give me the strength to keep going. I know hard times will make you wonder if God is there and if there is any real purpose to your life. I also know, without a doubt, the pain and suffering I endured was all a part of pushing me further

---

104 Proverbs 20:5

toward my purpose. I speak from experience when I say that everything happens for a reason, and it will ultimately push you toward your God-given purpose.

God has given us all the tools we need to be successful in living an intentional life and understanding our purpose. Yet too often, we live life aimlessly and settle for so much less using our circumstances as an excuse. Your life doesn't have to be boring or mundane or less, nor am I suggesting that you must save the world. What I am saying is if a significant portion of it is boring or mundane, then you are not living your life to your fullest potential, or you are going down the wrong path. Now don't get me wrong, I'm not saying life is going to be a bed of roses and everything is always going to smell, feel, and look good. What I am saying is, when you are living your life with purpose, the ugly times of life are easier to endure because you can constantly remind yourself that there is a bigger purpose for your life.

So then, why aren't you living an intentional, purpose-filled life? Why aren't you waking up excited and eager to challenge each day with drive and determination? I'm not going to act like I have all the answers. But what I can say is you must stop letting your past failures and current trials be an excuse for you to live small when God requires you to live BIG! When your heart is filled with grief and pain, when your mind is occupied with dismay, when life is bursting at the seams with chaos, and even when you are overcome with anxiety because everything is hitting you all at the same time, understand this, God IS moving you toward your purpose. During life's circumstances, God will not only reveal Himself to you but also you will begin to see your true self and your purpose.

GOD'S INTENTIONAL PLANS FOR YOUR PURPOSE

I know I said this before, but I'll say it again. "We know for those who love God all things work together for good, for those who are called according to His purpose."[105] This verse is not just a good Christian scripture but really means that the good, the bad, and the ugly will ultimately work itself out, even when you cannot see anything good in it. We have to hold fast to the promises of God that say, "The LORD God is a sun and shield; the LORD bestows favor and honor. No good thing does He withhold from those who walk uprightly."[106] This verse says that God won't withhold the blessings He has planned for you. Therefore, even in the midst of your losses, your pain, your grief, and the unknown, you can also know beyond a shadow of a doubt God is going to sustain you. The questions you have can only be answered through your life's story, so just remember your purpose is the reason you exist. You exist because God put you here for an intentional purpose, and that purpose is greater than you. Life is full of risks, so you can't be overly cautious about exploring your purpose. Truthfully, being overly cautious means you are operating in fear. When an opportunity is staring you in the face, it is not the time for fear but is time to take a leap of faith.

I am reminded of a story about a young girl named Joni Eareckson who went swimming in the Chesapeake Bay with her sister. Joni decided to dive into the clear water, not realizing the water was too shallow for diving. She smashed her head on a rock, severing her spinal cord, immediately making her a paraplegic. After this tragic accident, Joni endured painful and grueling rehab for many years. Over fifty

---

[105] Romans 8:28
[106] Psalm 84:11

Purpose

years later, Joni has never experienced a miracle from God allowing her to get up and walk. Her life-altering accident may seem to have ripped her life out of her hands. After all, Joni must depend on someone every single day of her life for the most mundane tasks like brushing her teeth, combing her hair, feeding and bathing herself, and even sitting up in her wheelchair. Does it seem like what has happened to Joni is unfair? How could such a loving God allow an innocent child to endure such a tragedy and such long-lasting adversity?

It is easy to be angry at God and blame Joni's continued suffering, or our own suffering, on God for not intervening. Maybe you are not facing a physical or mental disability, but are there any disappointments, let downs or series of events you have had to face that make you feel angry with God? What has happened that makes you question God in your despair, or demand Him to give you answers? Even though Joni is paralyzed and continues to struggle with additional health issues, she is still able to see the power of God in her life. Despite Joni's accident, she has found a way to find purpose and live intentionally even with her disability though her ministry Joni and Friends- Advancing Disabilities Ministry. Joni's life is a testimony, an inspiration and a source of encouragement to many people who live with physical disabilities. Therefore, I challenge you to have an open mind as you try to understand God's plan for your life even while emotionally paralyzed.

Your entire life has been deliberate, determined, calculated, designed, and intentionally purposed by God. The good, the bad, and the ugly you that have experienced in life is a part of God's plan, providing clues and opportunity to find your purpose and live it out. When your dreams and goals seem out of reach, place your faith in God. In fact, this is the time to get a double dose of faith because God is going to take you down an unexpected path to stretch you and to show you more fully your purpose in life. God will give you the hope and strength to continue to believe in your goals and believe in yourself even when it seems impossible. Your actions, your motives, and your plans have each been intentionally calculated and directed with God's delicate touch. Purpose, which is directed by God, is deeply rooted inside your soul, so it is up to you to dig it out and bring it to the surface.

Someone once asked me, "Adrianne what does it mean to live an intentional life with purpose?" I believe intentional living means you are living out your life with a daily purpose. Intentional living also means not only can you *see* God working in your life, but you also have a greater understanding of *how* God is working in your life just as Naomi did. To live intentionally and ultimately penetrate the world by maximizing your potential, you must be dedicated to persevering through pain and suffering, preparing for the journey, purification, restoration, and purpose. Let God show you what you can learn from your trials and perceived setbacks even amid your trying circumstances. Let God remove the self-doubt and increase your capacity to dream unthinkable dreams. Why? God has an intentional purpose and a plan just for you. When you seek God's direction, it allows you to have the freedom to express your own pain and empathize with others who have endured similar circumstances. It also allows you to be free to share with the world your life and your purpose because you decided to live an intentional life.

It's time to think about your passions and how they line up with your purpose. I want you to take intentional steps on this journey of purpose. I don't want you to miss out on being the best of the best at what God has planned for you to accomplish in your life. Bringing your purpose to the surface means understanding not just who you are but what value you have. You must seek Him to find it. You will have to surrender yourself to the signs and signals God has shown you throughout the years. If you still don't have a clue as to what your purpose in life is, then you need to figure out what is still holding you back. Are you still replaying your past failures over and over in your mind? Has a failed relationship paralyzed you from moving forward? Are you confined and in constant worry over your financial situation, not releasing yourself to trust God as your provider? Have you received an unfavorable health diagnosis? Is your focus being divided because your children's schedule or other time robbers have zapped your mental capacity to endure anything else? As you seek to fulfill your hopes and dreams, don't let days go by without having both the drive and purpose to accomplish it. Don't let anything hold you back any longer.

Will you trust Him to show you the way? God has let you feel His presence even when you felt alone. He sent you words of encouragement from a friend or even from a stranger when you were feeling down. He used someone to show you His love just when you needed it the most. Everything that has happened is intentional, and all these things are pushing you to understand your purpose. Therefore, it is time for you to review the course of your life, so you can see where God's hand has been present during all the chaos, the difficulties, the grief, the inconsistencies and even during times you lacked trust. The Bible says, "Count it all joy when you fall into various trials, knowing that the testing of your faith produces patience."[107] Praise God and trust Him with a crazy level of faith that doesn't match your circumstances. Let your joy bubble over and place your hope and faith in the LORD, so you can see your life as God sees it. Let me remind you that you are still standing, and God is still working. The Apostle Paul said he was, "hard pressed on every side, yet not crushed, perplexed but not in despair, persecuted but not forsaken, struck down but not destroyed."[108] Meaning, in spite of the issues he was facing, he knew he would get up and continue to persevere. So, get up and stand in front of the mirror and remind yourself to straighten up your crown! Remember who you are. You are a prince or princess of the King and your life is your testimony. You are a child of God, an heir to the throne, a co-heir with Jesus and you are Royalty!

I urge you this day to challenge yourself to live life intentionally. Make it a point to not let another day go by without living it with the intention to fulfill your purpose. Time heals all wounds, but what time cannot do is give back the time you have lost. Anyone can learn from their mistakes and live an intentional life, but no one can live a life filled with excuses and expect to reach their fullest potential. God has given you unique gifts to use and to share with the world. If you choose not to walk in purpose, you are robbing the world of the gift God has given you to give to us. And if you don't value your gifts, you will miss out on using them, or God may even take them away.

---

107 James 1:2-3 NKJV
108 2 Corinthians 4:9 NKJV

Intentionally living out your purpose requires a level of patience. Your aspirations and dreams will not happen overnight. Unfortunately, we have created a fast-food, microwave society that has abandoned the slow cooker and conventional oven for a quick result. In the 1980's the term "road rage" was coined because of people's lack of patience while driving. Angry and aggressive behavior toward other drivers to release frustration occurs all because of impatience. If you have ever worked in retail or in a customer service job, then you likely have experienced impatience firsthand. Impatient people often take out their frustrations on the employees for what they conceive as inconvenient wait times. Life is inevitably surrounded by waiting and timing, especially when it comes to living out your purpose.

Unfortunately, because we have gotten so accustomed to the speed of technology, online shopping, and our fast food society, we have forgotten how to wait, and more importantly how to wait on God. We want everything now, in fact, we wanted it yesterday. In terms of sports, if you jump the gun, it costs you a penalty or may even cost you the race. There is a reason why waiting on God is good when you are seeking out your purpose. If your life often feels like you have been sitting inside God's waiting room, then don't you worry. It is in the waiting room of life where you will have an amazing encounter with the LORD. It is in the waiting room of life where your character grows, you gain strength and your faith is increased. It is in the waiting room of God where you learn how to grow in your prayers, and you learn how to rely on God. If you are waiting to hear from God regarding a specific area in your life such as a new job, a companion, your marriage, a child, your health, or starting a new adventure, it is key to completely trust that God is listening. This does not mean your answer may not be delayed, nor may it always be what you were expecting. Nonetheless, the LORD is listening, and He will answer. Just remember there is a reason for all your waiting, and it will eventually point you toward a life of fulfillment and purpose.

The book of Proverbs says, "Commit your work to the LORD, and your plans will be established."[109] This means you must fully commit to God to live an intentional life; and when you commit to God, He will direct you down the right path to a life filled with purpose. I believe God has an intentional plan specifically for you to penetrate this world with the influence only you can give. It will take determination and dedication, and it will take hope which is just an extension of your faith. When you are overwhelmed and anxious is when you must dig deep into your faith and trust God to keep you moving toward your purpose. Although you may not know how things will turn out, continue to place your hope in Christ because His promises for you are true *and* intentional. "Blessed is the one who listens to Me, watching daily at My gates, waiting beside My doors. For whoever finds Me finds life, and obtains favor from the LORD."[110] Ask God to give you the ability to recognize and understand your purpose, then listen and wait for the guidance to know how to live intentionally.

When a man decides he is ready to marry his girlfriend, he may ask his friends what he should do for the proposal. Especially nowadays there are many YouTube videos and Facebook feeds with men and their unique proposals. He

---
109 Proverbs 16:3 NKJV
110 Proverbs 8:33-35 NKJV

proposes marriage because he is confident that he wants to spend the rest of his life with her and she might want to spend the rest of her life with him. The dictionary says that a proposal means "to offer or suggest for consideration, acceptance, or action: to propose a new method."[111] Well, today I propose or suggest for your consideration that you change your current method of thinking, so you can begin living intentionally toward your purpose. If it means you need to change directions because your life feels unfulfilled, then be intentional and change directions. If it means eliminating certain Negative Nancy's from your inner circle, then be intentional and take the steps to remove those people from your sphere of influence. If you need to modify your surroundings, then move into a different environment and change your mind by altering what you watch, listen to or read. Do some deep soul searching. Do whatever you need to do to get there emotionally and take steps toward living an intentional life to find your purpose.

---

[111] Proposal. In dictionary.com online dictionary. Retrieved January 8, 2018, from http://www.dictionary.com/browse/proposal

CONCLUSION

THROUGHOUT THE BIBLE, countless stories show how God intentionally intervenes in the world to accomplish His purpose. In each, God intervened with intentional miracles and astonishing works. God was intentional when He created the world in six days and rested on the seventh. God was intentional when He created Adam and crafted Eve from Adam's rib. God was intentional when He allowed the flood to destroy the world, yet Noah's family was spared. God was intentional when He brought Jesus into this world through the Virgin Mary fulfilling the prophecy of Jesus as the Messiah. God was intentional when He sent Jesus to the cross to die for our sins.

Intentionally living out your purpose is bigger than you. It requires that you take a leap of faith instead of sitting on the sidelines waiting for something to happen to you or for you. God wants your faith to be accompanied by action, so let your faith be actively working toward you living out your purpose. Proverbs says, "Many are the plans in the mind of a man, but it is the purpose of the Lord that will stand."[112] Trust that God's plan for your life is exponentially greater when you are walking in faith and obedience to His purpose. "For it is God who works in you, both to will and to work for His good pleasure."[113] Therefore, continue to seek God for His intentional purpose and plan for your life. Regardless of the obstacles you face, God's plan for you *is* intentional. Your perfect imperfections are perfect, so stop worrying about what others might think about you if you tried to start your own business, or if you decided to quit your job to take a leap of faith and follow your dreams.

If you will lean on God's strength, it is then that you will be able to work toward your purpose. So, what are you waiting for? What are you putting off because you thought it could not be done? Jump out *expecting* God to catch you and push you toward His intentional path for your life. He knows the plans He has promised for your life. When God gives you a promise, you can trust God is faithful to keep His promise. God's promises are true for our lives regardless of what is happening and what has occurred in the past because God's promises are based on His word and His perfect character. They are not based on our imperfect lives. Shelter, peace, provisions, health, ability, finances, employment, and your dreams are all in God's control.

So, keep persevering. The LORD is stretching you and showing you your purpose through the trials of your life. God will give you the hope and strength to continue to believe in your goals and even believe in yourself when it seems impossible. Your actions, your motives, and your plans have each been intentionally calculated and directed

---

112 Proverbs 19:21 NASB
113 Philippians 2:13 NKJV

with God's delicate touch. Just think about it, when you are focused on your trials, you cannot give the world your best. When you put your trials in God's hands, He will give you the ability to walk in your purpose, and He will give you peace in the middle of your storms. With God, nothing is hopeless no matter how difficult things may get. The questions you have can only be answered through your own life's story as your purpose is discovered. You exist in life because God put you here for an intentional purpose, and that purpose is greater than your current circumstances.

Don't let your past failures and current trials be an excuse for you to live small when God requires you to live BIG! God IS working behind the scenes moving you toward your purpose. I challenge you today to do more productive activities that push you toward your purpose. Spend time working on your purpose, your finances, your family and spend more time with God. Give Him your first, not your leftovers. The failures and setbacks you experience are your future's stepping stool. Learning from your failure will help you push yourself into bigger heights of greatness. Don't let your failures paralyze you and thrust you away from greatness because there is nothing that will happen that will catch God by surprise.

Although you may struggle with the outcome or the direction God has for you, keep your thoughts positive because God already knows your fears and anxieties. Just as God was intentional with the circumstances in the lives of Naomi, Ruth, Boaz and all the other Bible characters I mentioned, as well as the famous and historical individuals, God has an intentional purpose for your life. God was intentional when He chose you. God was intentional when He placed certain desires for your future inside of you. God did not create you as a failure, but a winner. Therefore, live intentionally and find your purpose even amid pain and suffering. Find your purpose when you are preparing for the journey. Find your purpose when you purify yourself and even while you are being restored. When you figure out what your purpose is, then you *will* find fulfillment and know, without even a shred of doubt, *"God's Intentional."*

BIOGRAPHY

ADRIANNE WATSON is a native of Cleveland, Ohio and has been serving the homeless, speaking, preaching, coaching and instructing Fortune 500 Companies, small businesses, non-profit organizations, and churches worldwide for over two decades nationally and internationally. She has a Bachelor of Arts degree in Communications from Case Western Reserve University and a Theology of Masters (Th.M.) degree in the areas of Systematic and Historical Theology from Dallas Theological Seminary. Adrianne has written two other books: *Broken Crayons Still Color – Overcoming Dysfunctional Relationships* and collaborated with nineteen other female authors who offer their personal testimonies in *Soul Talk Anthology.*

Adrianne started her ministry, Royalty Ministries, with a focus to encourage and engage women to help them overcome their trying circumstances as well as understand their purpose. Royalty Ministries has grown into an international social media organization that continues to touch the hearts of people of all ages and race through daily devotionals, homeless pampering events, and conferences. Adrianne is a Sr. Account Manager at RightNow Media Ministries and serves as a Leader of Life Group Leaders at Chase Oaks Church in Plano, Texas, under Senior Pastor Jeff Jones. She is happily married to Arthur Lee Watson, Jr., a native of Birmingham, Alabama. He is the Pastor of Adult Ministries at Chase Oaks Church and a student at Dallas Theological Seminary pursuing a Master's in Christian Leadership.

FOR MORE INFORMATION ABOUT ADRIANNE WATSON
AND TO BOOK SPEAKING EVENTS,
PLEASE VISIT WWW.ROYALTYMINISTRY.COM OR
EMAIL THEROYALTYMINISTRY@GMAIL.COM.

www.ingramcontent.com/pod-product-compliance
Lightning Source LLC
Chambersburg PA
CBHW050438010526
44118CB00013B/1591